I dedicate this collection of my WrathBliss

Prose & Poetical rendered Ramblings

To my close Friends & Family,

& to fellow Dreamers & Poetry readers everywhere-

We Dream, we strive, we try, we fall down, and we get back up,

We Live, We Love, We Inspire,

To create, to share…we so do desire,

And so, on & on we yearn-

Knowing that rejection, judgment….…..or possible acceptance

Could be lurking close by in the shadows,

Awaiting our very next attempt, our next failed turn,

To show a sign of our regression or our progression,

Even though we may have our concerns;

*Don't worry Dean…it isn't perfect.

It is still raw'n'flawed, riddled with some mistakes.

Still me distilled within these many pages of word & rhyme.

However, it is a better version than my previous II attempts…

With Imperfections, errors, mistakes that may still be found

By that reader willing to visually traipse through these pages

Written by a man…a dreamer..a human being, …not a robot;

Deep down, we all wish to be either unique, normal, abnormal, special, appreciated, valued..or not-

..More than less, while showing support & love to the rest…No matter what…

We must be ourselves… From our worst parts to our best. From our Magic…to our flaws.

Greetings Dear Reader,

I Welcome YOU to My Partial Memoir-ish Poetical Prose

Dark Strides III

(FINAL ATTEMPT)

(The Past & Present Battle within the Multiverse of Me &…More)

by

WrathBliss

Timothy Delbert McAllen

Aka Mr. Imagine the Author (Per my CL-Personals posting days)

+++Please Pardon All the ………………………dot dot dots & etc…+++

WrathBliss defined:

Wrath= A Central Optimistic/Pessimistic Passionate Fury &/or Way.

Examples: To Love with Fury. To experience a Furious Love.

I am Madly in Love with HER. Wrath is not always about anger.

Bliss= A Crucial Optimistic Passionate Delight, Joy, Harmony.

WrathBliss= the best & worst of all of me, myself & i.

With Wrath & Bliss through Life & Love I Wonder, I Wander, I Live;

My Dark Strides= My Obscure Progress.

A few possible silly to serious quotes by some possible past, present or imminent skimmers or readers….

Skimmer 1: "Another mumbo jumbo depressed poet that is all butt hurt

About his rough artistic plight, pathetic life & crap like that"-

Skimmer 2: "This is a collection of badly written wannabe poetry/prose with an abundance of

Grammatical errors. If I was grading this so called, "Work of Poetic Art"..I'd write a nice

BIG RED F- on all 3 editions of this fouled-up monsterpiece and be done!"-

Reader 1: "I think this guy is expressing like I wish I….could"+

PS: I dig De La Soul's- Me, Myself & I. Check out De La Soul for some dope Hip Hop-

1st Edition Originally Published on my Bday 1/30/2014

52 pages

2nd Edition Published 2/1/2015

2nd Revised Edition © 2010-2015 Timothy D. McAllen

124 pages

3rd Edition Published 2/16/2015

3rd Revised Edition © 2010-2015 Timothy D. McAllen

133 pages

The WrathBliss ™ ®

was created by & is the sole property

of Timothy Delbert McAllen

Concept/Cover art/Photographs/Editing/Design/Mistakes

by Timothy Delbert McAllen, Mr. Imagine the Author

I used Cooltext.com for awesome font/logo design.

I edited photos, front & back cover with Photoshop Elements 11.

WrathBliss Rambles - Dark Strides III Final Attempt 2015

Printed & bound by Lulu.com

LULU ISBN: 978-1-304-54812-2

ISBN 978-1-304-54812-2

Please visit, find, discover, contact, share, listen to, & read me @

wrathbliss.com
facebook.com/iamwrathbliss
facebook.com/wrathbliss

facebook.com/thewrathbliss
soundcloud.com/thewrathbliss

cdbaby.com/cd/thewrathbliss
to hear & purchase my debut MP3 EP Digital Album
youtube.com/wrathbliss
youtube.com/thesneatles

facebook.com/pianofunoodling
facebook.com/AmusingMusicLessons

Please also show Support & Visit
Denver.ClassicPianos.net
Angeloscds.com
schmittmusic.com
arapahoelibraries.org
doublescopefilms.com
Arcthrift.com
Goodwill.com
Cooltext.com

+ Personalized Poetry by WrathBliss is Also Available +
per YOUR request & a most delightful, supportive Donation... if applicable.

Table of Contents Dark Strides III - Final Attempt: ....For those that dare to read!

Fleeting GREETINGS

I'll get right to the point...

This is my 3rd & Final Attempt at self-publishing

My 1st book of Memoir-ish Poetical Prose & Beyond; a collection of writings

That I call....Dark Strides.

You may find them to be absurd, redundant, odd,

or beautiful & excitingly inviting.

Whether that sounds like some confidence lacking pathetic excuse or not...

"I am only human after all.......

I am only ME after all,

I am flawed after all, ..or I'd be a God after all......"

...lol.

Yes...I did it my way...I wrote it my way, including my flaws, my beauty & all.
Bad or Good...it's just a book introducing my dark, my light, my heart, my soul
& rhyme; ENJOY!...Redundancies & All!

-None the less, none the more, this is a treasure trove of unique
poetical ramble-ized prose regarding: personal struggle, opinions,
thoughts, failures, fears, insights, concerns, dreams, flaws, beauty,
philosophicals & beyond.

ENJOY!

Useless or Useful Bonus Information & Mission Statement

Some other titles that I had in mind …until **Dark Strides** came to be…

Things Written In Personal Crisis

Therapy Using Redundancy & Rhyme

I Battle I, to Live, to Breath, to Survive,

Let It All Out B4IDIE….or….So I Don't Die With All This In Me—

For I CHOOSE & have CHOSE

To Inspire People To Express What They Feel With Heart on Sleeve through Poetic Prose-

Poems About Me, My Thoughts, Failures…That You Might Not Care To Know

The Redundant Poet & His Book Full of Problems, Issues, Failures, Repair

This Could Suck, Find Another Book Asap

What if You Read this book & life IT

It is what IT is, it is not what IT is not

My First Pathetic Attempt at Publishing My Horrid Poetry

A Doubtful Progression of Poetic Prose

Striding Through My Good, Bad & Ugly Poetry

At War With Myself, While Trying To Survive Life

Uniquely Dark & Strange Poetically Charged Rambles

Wandering Through the Wide World of Wrath & Bliss Within

Out of 510 Facebook invites to Buy my 2nd attempt, only 2 did so, Bummer!

The MISSION STATEMENT

I shall keep striving on, dreaming, living, trying, creating, sharing…….
COME FEVERISH FEAR OR INFAMOUS FAMINE,

WHAT EXISTS WITHIN THESE PAGES

ARE FOR YOUR EYES TO HOPEFULLY

OPEN MINDEDLY & MOST HAPPILY EXAMINE,

UNLESS ALL YOU DISCOVER DOES NOTHING BUT MADDEN,

FOR I WON'T APOLOGIZE FOR BEING

EMOTIONALLY & EXPRESSIVELY flawed & human, AND QUITE

POSSIBLY…REDUNDANTLY…YET..BEAUTIFULLY….LADEN;

Brief Bio Informatives about me, myself & I:

Born in the state of Texas, Year of 71'. High School Grad', Class of 89'Wildcat/Eagle.
Never into cig smoking. Drank a bit of booze from my teens to mid 20's.
Tried some pot in my early twenties. 6x total. Discovered that drugs weren't
For me…due to me being so rather, Naturally High!
I've worked many jobs through the years. Stay at home parenting
Being my most important & meaningful job.
I'm happy to no longer be out there single & searching.
I am in a committed relationship with a wonderful woman that I love very much.

My father was a proud Vietnam Veteran Soldier. He passed away
Feb. 21, 2003. He was handfed many meds for his various
Physical, PTSD, liver, psychological issues…care of the VA.
He was depressed about his health, life, past, & illness'.
He lost the willingness & strength to try, to persevere, to live.
I tried to inspire him. I tried to show him how important he was.
How important life was. How much we cared for him.
No matter how our relationship was before his illness' swept
Him up, wearing him down, both his body, mind…& temper,
I know he did his best with what he had. I miss YOU Dad……

My mother is alive & enjoying adventures with her friend Dean & others, along
With her 5 loveable dogs. I am very happy for her indeed. Love YOU Mom!

Sept. 2007 I moved to Denver, CO, to be closer to my daughter D.
I have been in numerous bands since my late teens. I dance okay.
I love my family, music, life, making people laugh, inspiring
Thought, chance, playing acoustic guitar, Piano, giving beginner
Music lessons as a hobby-job, writing of course, dogs, cats, living.
+ I dig songwriting, doing amateur standup comedy & improv sketch comedy.
My diverse collection of music is almost as big as my heart. I LOVE MUSIC!
I have dreams…like many. I have issues…like many. I am grateful to be alive.

An
OPEN INVITATION

…If you stop here…

So much indeed…you will surely miss-

So I invite you to fully or minimally experience these Dark Strides of WrathBliss;

If need be, forget following a table of contents,…

Live a little, LIVE A LOT..take a chance, take a dive,

For you are Beautiful, Intelligent & Alive!

Just GO FOR IT…TURN to a page & start reading, skimming,

It is your choice. Your time here, within these pages

I will appreciate none the less, no matter how long you gravitate

Over my poetical offerings.

I promise YOU that you are safe. Nothing will jump out & harm you.

These are words after all. Not bullets & blades seeking a target.

Perhaps something may very well catch your attentive sense & excite you!

Once & a while, living without a map, without a plan,

Can be an inspirational delight, allowing us to escape from our own issues.

So…….

Feel free to thumb through these pages blindly……

And if by chance YOU find something

Amusing & viable that YOU might so kindly

Enjoy reading daily..or nightly….dimly or brightly…

Here is your chance to discover <u>something</u> unique that will move thee,

Honest, muddled, emotional, frenzied, cantankerous offerings that are

Possibly dull, beautiful, ridiculous, redundant, romantic, repugnant,

Written, expressed, suggested, confessed with lawless poetic conviction

And with the best of intentions…

by me, Timothy.

Warning, Disclaimer, Excuses I

If you've troubled to thumb through a few pages thus far,…
You might possibly be thinking something like…
"What is this CRAP? Poetry? A nonsensical attempt at being expressive?
Or mere mumbo jumbo mamble jamble Rambles?"

Though I fear that there are a few unlike them, unlike those
That might think the worst of this haphazardly expressed wordy mess,
I know deep down in my heart of hearts that
There could possibly be a few… myself included..that deem
This collection of writings…to be…
Nothing more than a collection of abnormal, un-uniform poetically
Profound expressives, with a touch of flawful messisness
With just enough deplorable amounts of self-deprecative uncanniness
Combined with a sufficient level of meloish-dramatic poeticness
To present one or a few readers with an interestingly viable read….
If such a read is desired before your read time doth expire;

What IS THIS? (Sarcasm or Truth)
A mess of words that YOU will love or hate, enjoy or resist?
Could this be some raw style of something that is more than nothing?
Written by a new breed of poet, like Me, Myself & I….
Soulfully packed full of poetically streamed
Thoughts, pains, worries, dreams & some sensually expressive things….
All being possibly so very grammatically incorrect & visually obscene?

Most definitely...my answer is…: YES!…
My 2nd answer is: NO…
My 3rd answer is: Quite Possibly!..that IT could be! That IT is, what IT is!
This is what you feel that it is. This is what I did, like it or not.

For IT is….for THIS is…simply what IT is..or was. No more, no less.

Here is where I should digress, to express less. But I won't..I do confess.

Whether you care to Like it, Love it or Undeniably…HATE IT…,

Skim it, read it, …or blatantly Trash it..

Praise it …Bash it, Compare it…or Share it….

It is what IT is, remaining as IT is…until IT is no longer;

Yes…conjure up a standing ovation for FREEDOM of SPEECH!

That is the GREAT thing about FREEDOM/ aka the Art of Expression.

Freedom of expression,

Freedom to try, Freedom to INSPIRE…

Freedom to Live, to Give, to Create, to Share…

Before we are Free to Die….

For you, for WE are Free….until we are no longer, unless we never were,

Free To do, to chance, to discover…

To freely run as far from these vast pages

As fast as humanly possible…whilst I freely, humbly rumble tumble

With words on page, rambling on & on, through dark dusk to lit dawn;

(Read these pages while sipping red wine, coffee, tea, water, juice, cocoa, while
soaking in a warm bath, while lying in bed, seated on a train, at a coffee shop, on
your couch, at the park, before a blind date & etc.)

No matter what…all politics, opinions, self-depracative factors, flattery, chit-chattery aside…

Thank YOU for YOUR consideration & time,

Whether you read inside or outside, Enjoy the read, Enjoy the ride!

WELCOME I &/or Warning II:

Welcome to my **WrathBliss** Rambles.

The reduxed & revised version of my assorted writings, old & new, including

Redundancies, deprecatives & etc., edit III, the Final Attempt.

This that I have deemed in name as the, as my: **DARK STRIDES,** Partial Memoir-ish Poeticals.

Where my flaws & beauty embrace where my Darkness & Light collide,

Dreams, opinions, fears, doubts & all,

Within these poetically rambled expressive writings,….

Some average, some exciting, some absurd,

Found within, within these lines,

These sentences that I chose to form with the art of expression, the power of words

…horrid as they might just be, they were formed by little old non-degreed..High School

Graduate of 1989—ME!

So be forewarned,

It is when ONE stops doing what they LOVE,

That which they enjoy, that which is a great part of them,

Losing their passion, their drive,

No longer DREAMING, TRYING, LIVING, battling….

Only existing to merely survive….

That is when they should then be saved…reminded….or sadly mourned;

YES…this is,…
Not my most romantical offerings BY FAR.
Not my most optimistical offerings at all.
Nor are these writings my worst……but….possibly some of my best…(dot..dots….& all).

That is, once you get past all the blah-blah redundancies

That are mere signs of my curved & fluctuating confidence level,

Battling it out like Angel & Devil within that Multiverse of Me;

-I hope you had a beautiful day, at school, at work, at play-

More Dedications & Titanicalicious Thanks:

This collection of expressive rambles is also dedicated with Love to:
My Lovely Love- O. Michelle B.: Thank YOU so much for your patience,
understanding, love, being a wonderful mommy, being a great friend,
For the many hours to write & edit, & for everything else my darling!
My Lovely daughter DeLanna R.: Live-Love-Dream-Dance-Draw-Inspire!
Our very cute son Finn Timothy…whom joined us on 9/6/2014.
I wish you a full & wonderful life filled with love, joys & followed dreams.
Thank you all for sharing your love, & this short, beautiful life with me!
My lovely mother Genivee R.M.: Thank you for my life & everything else!

Happy Birthday (2/18) Dean! Thank you for your inspiring feedback per
My 1st edition & beyond; for your kindness; for being a wonderful
& loving friend to my lovely mother. You are Appreciated!

Thank God, Allah, Your God, My God, OUR GOD, Earth, the Aliens,
Respect, Peace, Love, Understanding, Humanity… & the Powers that Be;
RIP: My dad Johnny D. M., Aunt Rose, Grandma Eva Rod.,
Joey Cabrales, Martin Luther King Jr., Mohandas Karamchand Gandhi,
Nelson Mandela, John Lennon. YOU ARE REMEMBERED & MISSED!

My long time Best Friend/X-Bandmate **Jaime Blanco**(Happy Feb. Bday!)& Family & his
Doublescope Films, Ann Gulbrandsen., Jennifer D.G, Mark Tony Torres,
Josh & Angel & the Cabrales Family, All of my SA Texas/Germany Fam,
The Dreamers, the Readers, Those that Inspire, goodhearted soldiers & police,
Peacekeepers, lifesavers, all goodhearted people. Thank you All!
The life/love/laughter/inspiration & music that I have discovered,
Created, shared & been inspired by on my journey, from then to now
& beyond, **Paula Moses Hoang** & her beautiful family- for buying my 1st ed.,
& for your support/donation to my digi-Piano fund & for your Kindness,

13

Brian Oakley & Madison- for being Kind, Cool & Supportive.....
& for the first to buy my 2 cd (now discontinued) + 1 book bundle,
Bob "Pianist" Baker for the piano time, kindness & pianospiration,
Dino & Ray & staff @ Schmitt Music for the piano time,
Don West & Chris Ranney & all at Classic Piano on Broadway-
For the piano practice & recording time,
Jesse Bubbles E, Angel/Rix Gonzalez & our InvasI band days,
Because we still Rock! All of my music students especially my bestest
Most creative student of all-Madison,
Thank you Matt & the Johnson Family for the teaching opportunity!
Kat, Cathy, Donna, Ann, & all @ Cherry Creek Retirement Village!
My past co-workers @ Wellbridge: Diane, Eileen, Colleen, Judy,
Kristi, Fred, Melinda..Thank you for 5 & ½ years of Cube Life
comradeship! Sonny Nicks for your words of wisdom & inspiration telling
me to keep trying, striving, dreaming, creating, sharing & thriving.

THANK **YOU**_____!

(Please write your name on line above)

YES...MANY THANKS to YOU!

Best wishes to YOU & YOUR FAMILY!!

FOR YOUR SUPPORT, BELIEF, DONATION,

KINDNESS, RESPECT, PURCHASE & ASSISTANCE!!

FOR **YOU** ARE PRICELESS & TRULY APPRECIATED.

Wishing YOU the very best on YOUR journey

In & Of

Life, Understanding, Dreams, Goals, Discoveries,

Romance, Health, Peace & Love;

14

Digs that I DIG:

Yolanda's Tacos are Titillatingly YUMMY!

Angelo's Cds - Marcel, Angelo, Julox & staff are Totally Awesome!

Goodwill & ARC are Wonderfulicious!

Schmitt Music is Smashingly Superbulous!

Classic Piano Company on S. Broadway is Fantasterrifical!

Second Spin on Colorado Blvd. is Splendidacious!

Double Scope Films of El Paso, Texas is the Bestocious!

Homestead for the Cooltastic website tools!

Tattered Cover is Grandtabulous for supporting indie authors!

Colorado Public Radio…NPR is Divinistic!

The BookBar is Righteousissimo!

Twist & Shout is most Opulenticulous!

Mercury Café is most Magnificadora!

Lulu.com is so very Motivationally-Inspirationally-Brilliant!

Smoky Hill Library is Wondertastical!

WELCOME II

Welcome to IT, my Internal Trappings, my ideological trimmings,
Welcome to MY Dark Stride Happenings, my self-publishing beginnings,
Welcome to where I Testify that I am poetically Alive & Exacting,
With my feelings in the form of words, & how I tenderly extract them,
Welcome to that which is this vividly, imperfectly, slightly perfectly
Expressively expressed part of Me,...The Thinker, the Writer-reacting-

WELCOME to my dark & glowing long winded rambunctious Rambles,
Welcome to my meaningful missives, my nonsensical Epistles,
Welcome to where I write & share myself inside of vertical rectangles
With words that share my heart, my mind, my soul, my world, my flaws,
Not held back, not held down by any writing rules, policies or laws-

For I am more than just that villain poet anti-poet,
For I am more than just that tragic un-super, un-hero-esque zero,
More than
That partial loathing man with doubts, frustrations, flaws & fears,
That fool I am, that fool I've been throughout my many years,
That man that could've been a better friend,
That dreamer racing until the very end,
That man I am from A to Z, with a list of internal ingredients
That range from the best to worst of particles within & outside of me,
With self-deprecation occurring ever so naturally,
Something you might have already noticed if you did so choose to read
These here poetically blunderous lines that my heart chose to bleed,
Learning quickly..that nothing will come, nothing will ever grow
If you don't take the time to nurture yourself, or to plant your seed-

For you cannot enjoy your rise to the mountain peak
If you haven't battled it out with yourself & the world in the valley,
For it is within the valley that dreams do start,
Right where my heart & soul at times do fall apart,
To once again rally on, marching on, keeping on, believing, on & on,
With shield, with sword, with heart on sleeve…
I do my best to ensure that I can & will & do still believe
In dreams, ….even when I find it hard to believe in me-

Welcome to my expressive release & beyond, obscurities & all,
For on these pages I courageously rise & fall through adversity & all,
I march on to keep on keeping on, insecurely & securely standing tall….
And at times, I still find myself being temporarily trapped, still just me,
In that very cold misty, musky midst of my own mundane undertow,
Altering my path, stifling my way while stumbling through my day,
Still…just me…myself & I…
Trying to get along while paying dues, while paving my way-

Complaining as I do at times….through my each & every crisis
Whilst being wrapped up in my several <u>circumstancive</u> vices….
Admitting that my blunders, misfortunes & mistakes were not
Caused by anything other than my own
Contemporary coincidental circumstantial circumstances,
In addition to those turbulently moving, loud crashing waves around me,
That I do so experience on those rather
Stressful days of self-destructive dissatisfaction, distractions, infractions,
Disenchanted with me, myself & I, along with my poor choices & actions;

Some actions that were genius,
Some actions that were foolish,
Some actions that were possibly unkind,
Some innocent, some malevolent, some blind…
Some dumb, deaf, complicated & disjointed,
Some rather poignantly clear-

Some caused by temporary moments of ignorance,
Some caused by my own feverish depths of fear-

So, Here be I, Here I am,
Partly blessed, partly damned…
Owning up to my many colorful accomplishments & failures,
One at a time, rhyme by rhyme, each a possible derailer,
For this life I live is mine to live, mine to share, with love & loving care,
Whilst I fill these pages line by line, proving that I am most certainly,
A most obviously flawed one of a kind of the expressive kind-
And I know this life is not always fair,
For not every poem is meant to rhyme,
Not every poem is perfectly constructed, precise in metered time,
& I so do apologize with sadness
For being a burden of caused frustrations some of the time,
To HER, my Love, my fulltime Irish dove, my forever Valentine,……
My mate of Heart & Soul,
My Everything, My Garden… My Wild Rose…
You are why & where my seed of love is today,
So strong & true it grows,
Right where my Heart calls Home,…right beside you;

Though at times.., I am caught up in that which keeps me struggling
Unable to finally get ahead, thinking of myself as some arduous soul,
Like a plague, existing, rambling around with a curse over & upon me,
Knit within that thin fine fragile fabric of my fluctuating confidence,
Constructed with a constricted grip around my dreams, my life, my world,
Only wanting the best for me & my family, my love, my boy, my girl,
As I do hope & wish to soon be free from those various vile parts of me
Where self-deprecative tendencies are found so very naturally, internally..
& once again…please do pardon my ridiculous knack for redundancy;

And though I may suffer from that which keeps me cycling
Through my own expressive pitch black forest of redundancies…
I contest, I protest, I confess that I am at least…most happily free…
Or at least wishing to be Free…..

Free…
from those flaws that strangle I, hold me back, weigh me down,
Free…
from that which has me feeling rather ridiculously rooted at times,
Free…
from the dark reaches of my vague excuses & rancid reluctance,
Free…
from that daily struggle in that War between Me, Myself and I,
      Where my woeful Wrongs battle my rugged Rights,
          Where my damned Darkness battles my laudable Light,
And in the midst of all that rivalrous chaos
Between me & each of my striding sides…
I understand that I am perceived by many as being no more
Than some obscurely strange oddball guy that can be easily overlooked,
Though feeling perceived as such could mean that I'm very much in touch
With feeling like a loser from time to time, feeling so very unadorned-

And through all of that mumbo jumbo self-expressive ruckus…
I still find myself striving for such & such & that much more,
Reaching for some sort of strategic & important inner Change,
Spending time that I mustn't deplore while I continue to self-explore,
Though I admit, with strained tragic redundancy, I am flip'n StRaNgE,
And I continue to find myself in a sustained struggle from within
As my own worst enemy,..& my own worst capitulated friend,
Battling Between Me, Myself and I, on that tragic battlefield called LIFE..
Trying to believe that I am more than just another garrulous guy
Trying to end that tumultuous cycle of me VS i once again,
Caught up in a counterintuitive conflict that I may never truly ever win,
Admitting admittedly, repeatidly… that at times…
Through the action, the drama, the melodrama, I do unhappily descend,
Though certainly doing my best to fin on & on,
With a zealously resilient desire to gladly ascend B4 I waste my final dawn;

Wondering if this is really the extent of my poetical expressive expression.
Is it? Should I know? Will I ever admit it?
If this is my big DREAM…should I pack up & simply quit it?
Because so far, these pages are no more than
Merely mere meaningless poo to you, or you, or you, or me, or not?

Or is it all just the sum of some self-deprecative, suggestionated goo,
That I so do capriciously defend while writing this,
Yo-yoing as I do, entrenched in this wildstyled mess of words
Typed upon pages by a flawed son, man, a floundering flagrant fool
With thoughts & words to share & carelessly…semi-carefully unspool,
Writing more than less instead of following the rules & playing it cool
For a smorgasbord of nonexistent readers, maybe one or a few
That might find something here worth a read or a skim or two,
Being them barely a few VS those that might care to disapprove of

These words…that I poetically have spewed across pages, for me, for you,

Written by a fool that believes that he just might be unique enough

To be a diamond in the rhyme of rough with all the right & regal stuff..

Or merely a man that writes like shelves gather dust, pointlessly,

Like a street gathers litter, like abstinence gathers lust,

Like war continues on, while leaving nameless bodies unburied, unjust-

Forgetting about those many misplaced, broken families, shattered hearts,

Those people left to rebuild while war machines are left to rust,

So..failed analogy & all,…..what I am getting at…is this…

I am an expressive spirit, write on write I, to write I must,

Before tragedy overcomes me, before I arrive at my final dusk-

Here write I, onward, with goals & promises to keep,

Writing nothing more than words that seep

From my open inner wounds like pondered pus,

Wondering which one of us

Should be experiencing more signs of boredom &/or disgust….

And if you stop reading, stopping here…….

I'm sure that your reason or reasons…are & were viably just,

As I continue writing, because for me this is Live or Die.. Write or Bust,

Life or Death, ashes to ashes, dream, create, share or gather dust,

Do something about it, or just give up, this war contraption will not rust-

Win, Lose, LIVE…and share your heart, mind & soul, because I must…

So I'll write on & on, at times…lacking confidence, hope..& trust…

This I vow,..

Until my final break of **dawn**….(Another Prose related Poetic Redundancy)

As I share being vulnerable & insecure with those few that so dare

To tread on, read on, spending minutes on these pages, by dusk, by **dawn**,

Hoping for me to quickly eradicate my awful somber to sanguine state

While experiencing a fresh new peachy **dawn** of future & fate….

While I wrestle with the evidence of me being the opposite of demure,
Unable, possibly..incapable,..or simply unwilling to grasp that our society
Is very much more interested in that which is defined as "Less is More"-
So,….share I with you…my own expressive version
Where "More is Best"…at least for me,…
Dare I not be so engrained in owing you grandiose apologies
Regarding my ..perhaps, unimpressive written ways that are found
Within these poetic rambles, where I dare to confess, professing my way
Through my Dark Stride ramblings in this Dark Hearted Race called Life,
Carefully…lighting my way through this dark place of peril & strife…….
Using words as candles, lighting my way thru another page, another day,
Expressing, releasing myself to save myself from internal decaying dismay
While making my way through tumultuous tides of Life & Love,
Experiencing traces of good fortune & minor catastrophes…
Acknowledging that I AM so very awfully
Blessed to be ALIVE, sharing my life with those that depend on me
While I do my best to enjoy each breeze, each wave… of happiness
With confidence & insecurity deeply latched on my lucid wings,
With my ever so substantial array of self-doubts, fears & flaws
Stacked upon my back along with the weight of the world,
I will not bow to my weakness', I will march on, I will persevere…
Finding sweet solace in writing as I do,
Therapeutic as it is, here sit I silently at 3am, with no need to flap my jaws
When I can type with my ninja like fingers,

    Sparing the world the sound of my voice….

        Directing, releasing, sharing emotions

            Like herding herds of words

                OUTWARD….

Hopeful…that one day, these many preciously expressed sentences

Will be at least momentariously, visually & emotionally observed…

And thus, finally Appreciated, whilst being absorbed & Inwardly heard…

Be them received as beautiful…or nothing more than blatantly absurd,

Written by a man that is more than a ramblin' expressive, pleading nerd

Needing to deal with his own internal flaws, reality, the world & its laws

While kneading the dough & sharing the crust of his Heart, Mind & Soul-
(Is that redundant enough?)

Being the ONE against the gun, against the grain,

While Dealing with the Devil & his Un-merry band of Sinners

Whilst facing those self-purported painful doubts, fears & flaws,

Feeling that

I,

Knowing that

I…..

EXIST, is not enough,

For I must share my bewildered beauty & my unfavorable flaws

Feeling like I am the greatest

At being the greatest holder of the shortest straw

That anyone has ever seen or saw….

With what seems like nothing more

Than bad poetic blood coursing through my veins

In a Head on collision with myself,

Crashing, feeling like I'm rather nose diving into a bloody chainsaw,

With my pride trickling, or rather, quickly tumbling down at my side,

I find the time to write instead of committing a tragic suicide of silence

Where my fingers, voice, heart, soul & mind are no longer in residence

With my emotions..or this world any longer..

For I must stand up even on my weakest day to be stronger, blessed be…

I do pray there is hope for this self-deprecative, self-conscious me-

For I forge on with words flowing un-specifically prolifically

Writing with great persistence,

At War Within the depths of my greater resistance

Whilst trying to believe in my own expressive relevance

While coming to grips with the fact that I am nothing more,

Nor nothing less…….

Than an unknown ordinary commonplace poet,

Redundantly cursed, poetically blessed…

With nowhere warm nor safe to hide myself from my own degradation,

With nothing more than empty pages to fill with spicy burning thoughts

That I must purge every now & then, with words of faith, words of sin,

Before they rot, before they are lost

In Time's maze of graves, covered by cobwebs & moths,

Withering away in solitudes frost

For to finally say, "I'm Finally Published",

Comes with quite a humbling cost,

Even if the time taken to write this book of words

Is nothing more than a huge & blatant loss;

Though Grateful I am to no longer feel forever single & damned,

No longer writing about feeling lonely, living life unloved,

Accepting that my first marriage was fated to arrive at an end

So that I could start anew & finally find my O, my loving M.-

That friend that is my One & Only True Love now,

Yes…she was fortunately found,

For I may no longer have romantic missive based posts to share

Where single mingle Craigslist lady fans flock to read & stare

At men advertising their laundry list of ego, wants & needs

Or men like me that posted their heart on sleeve

Regarding their quest for true love unfound,

With words that were received as sincerely honest & profound…

For there..in that place.. I no longer must arrive seeking someone

To share love, to share life..as my lover, as my wife…

For SHE was found indeed..my dreams I surely did exceed….,

Yes.., Thankfully, the ONE I dreamed of,

The ONE I wanted & needed,

The mother of our son,

My One & Only True Love,

My kinky Moon, My splendid Stars,

My soothing Sun above;

So……..

…No longer write I of true love sought & unfound

With my valued free time,

For I do have other ills & joys to share in flawful written rhyme,

That keepith my heart stretched out over every word, line by line,

Written by…this man made of flesh & bone,

No longer seeking that thought of HER, no longer alone,

Though, I'm deduced at times by those things that still can bring down

That antiquated boy within me that resides at times inside a foolish clown

Of humorous dashing spirit that can be more annoying than fun & sound

While learning to accept me she does so very well,

Accepting my heaven along with my frustration causing hell…

Making the best & worst of IT, Right side up and/or upside down of IT

Be this a waste of words, or rather…something more implicitly profound,

For it is up to you…to continue reading for something that will astound,

Or to simply…put this little book I wrote safely on the ground;

The truth is…no matter how many skeptics or critics

That come & go, we must keep on keeping on…

So, Stand up, be strong,…

Know that we are a society that makes or breaks people,

We suggest, we highly rate, we denounce people…

Each of us a Judge, each group of us a jury,

My peers, strangers, friends, family, readers, thinkers, dreamers,

Haters, Lovers, and EVERYONE & EVERYTHING in between

Including all those middle of the road In-betweeners…

Making and breaking spirits along the route of our days,

Coldly, boldly admitting that we should give it up or continue on

Our path of dreams & more,

And out of those fortunate few of us that are found & explored…

Only one or two of us might be supported & adored,

While the rest of us find our home upon the cutting floor…

To write …I love,

To write …I do…

And though I love to write, whether what I write is liked or not,

It matters to me that I share this book of mine with You,

You the Judge, You the Jury, You…the witness of my Blissful Fury;

No matter what you choose or chose,

No matter what your choice was or will be,

Welcome…..to my Dark Strides…the progress of me, myself & I…

Each page possibly filled with what could be nothing more than

Pathetic poetic prose-ish rambles & skewed..sweet & soured redundancies

As you've witnessed, read & seen,….

Or, as a matter of fact…

You might find it to be….rather….

Something more than that,

Perhaps..something that you'll find to be a beautifully

Worthwhile & minimally confusing brand of idiosyncratic poetry…

Never the less…it is more than less

An assortment of my worst to best,

Written & expressed by this dear Wrathblissy man named Timothy;

Wagers of War

We all wage war someway, somehow,

Within the markets, within the world, within ourselves,

Within our hearts, our minds,

We are the Wagers of War-

On Land, on shores, on streets, behind doors,

For vengeance, for spoils, to settle our scores,

For something that is better,

For something that is more,

We are no stranger to War,

& even though We know the dangers of War

Still...

We are the Wagers of WAR....

Some Wage War with good intentions,

Some Wage War with bad intentions,

Some intentions are so very greedy, dark, evil, conniving & brutal,

A world at war, a self at war.......When will we learn that War, is so very futile-

Some battle with such passionate conviction,

Battling for change, battling themselves,

Battling over power, battling over dreams,

Battles between our best to worst friends & enemies,

Wars that take place externally,

As we see occurring daily in our society,

Wars that take place internally,

As we see by the struggles that we each face daily,

Just as I have battled within I, myself & me,

A war, a battle, a conflict within, that I do hope will one day end,

As I also hope & pray that we may soon stop battling within our Society;

Naked in the Darkness of Dream & Fantasy

Her naked body beside me, in the dead of the night,..
HER body…YOUR body—unlike anyone, unlike any BODY,
Both of us, alive with warmth,
Lying divided, swimming in charming night-dream revelations,
Entering obscene dreamstates, suggestively, separately,
A sweet calm collides with sweaty sour schemes
Whilst yet another argument between us aggravated our cohesive core-
If only we were able to touch, make-up, come back,
Come together….once more-

And soon we will,
And soon we did,
For that explains our human connection,
More meaningful than any bodily erection,
Safe we are for we both have grand bullshit detection…
Living in, living out Our human experience,
Being that WE are both rational & delirious,
Spirited & serious, explicable & mysterious…
Yet tragic,
Yet beautiful…
It is……. what we consider to be….most importantly……

…………………………O
……………………………U
………………………………R. ….Reality…
O
u
r………………………………………..…………….RELATIONSHIP…

Our relationship,

Our Spell, our time together, our history, our mystery,

Our Past, Our Present, Our Future, Our Love, Our Fury,

While surviving & enduring storms & all types of emotional weather,

Making the most of what we have within us, between us..with pleasure,

So that we may explore & enjoy this life, this love..entwined Together-

That which we are blessed with, that which we've found..Together...

That which we share, which we give, take, want, need, embrace,

For that spells out...OUR United Intoxicative UnIty,

Romantically, Spiritually & Sexually...

That sweet overflowing, ever present UnIty of You & Me...

Our understanding...our Treasure,

Our Love....& Our blessed FAMILY-

Be US, Girl & Boy, Woman & Man, Me & the One I do adore

With our lovely loving Family that includes 3 or 4,

Thank YOU for being here with me!

You are the Love of my Life, Dreams & my Reality,

For I wish not to battle in the darkness with silence & distance,

At war with your annoyance, frustrations & resistance...

I only wish to enjoy Our time as Lover, as Friend, woman & man

No longer divided down narrow cold lines between body & hand,

For I Love you...and I will do my best to understand,

Aware of your wants, your needs, as much as I possibly can;

The SINGer SONGWRITer that I was & never was, and will always be......

What I never was, what I'll never be
Because dreaming was easy,
Yes, dreaming is free,
It's those failed dreams
That hurt so painfully,
Wondering if I tried hard enough,
Or doubting whether or not I ever had the right stuff,
For perhaps it was never meant to be,
I know I tried to believe in what could be
There was still something that never went right for me,
And that could very well have been the wrong of me & mine,
A victim of a self-made outcome due to a weak heart & mind,
A fool that thought he was capable, yet culpable for not getting there
To that somewhere that I thought I did belong in song & soul,
To follow dreams can be a frantic foolish cold sport
That any proper person would so quickly abort....
But not I...not me...even if I am the dreamer
With too many dreams that would surely never be-

What I am...or what I was, still believing that I'll have my day,
For I won't give up just because LIFE has its dues & tolls,
For dreaming is priceless & free
Especially when you follow your
Dreams, seeing them through,
Even if-
Though, while I followed one dream in minimal capacity,
I filled the air with the sound waves of my heart.......
With melodies, words, rhymes, rhythms......
Guitar & or piano as my instrumental foundation

With my so-so vocal abilities standing out upon that music I created,
Nervously standing with negligible confidence
As I felt so very saturated with flaws & imperfections,
This artist within this man,
A singing man...
Singing my heart, sharing my soul, unveiling my insecurities,
Up against the best that adversity had to offer,
With obscurities curse coursing through the vein of my dreams-

I sing to ears too busy to listen, I sing to ears deaf to my sound,
Wishing that I possessed talent that was truly that beautifully profound,
Playing & singing, creating & sharing, to at least hear myself,
Reminding myself that, "I do exist." That I do matter. That I am Alive,
Living, breathing, dreaming through the noise & chaos of Life & Death,

Through the trials of my yesterdays, todays & tomorrows,
With meshed amounts of optimism, pessimism, strength & fear,
Swirled through & through with hints of happiness & sorrow
Like a recipe of my feelings wrapped up in my own wall of sound,
Possibly...unheard..unfelt by you...that supposed listener,....

& though my songs may very well not mean much to you,
Beautiful flaws, beauty, colors & truth can be found in each & every line,
Each unheard song being my own personalized musical design;
...Following dreams is as much a choice...as it is a fight,
Such has been my experience, my story, ...& sadly, such is my plight;

If you don't try, if you don't work at it, if you don't commit,
Life simply passes you by...
And that older you...will surely have to deal with it,
For even I am trying to get it right,

Complaining, merely talking about it.. surely doesn't accomplish it,

Only actions can do that.......

Even though I sing to an empty room,

Even though I write to no obvious market of readers

With no massive following awaiting the release

Of my expressive offerings of song, of word…

& though there are very few concerned & interested ears & eyes,

But if I quit now, I'll be the one regretting that I never…really tried,

Living a life with a fate denied,

Or….am I nothing more than a dreaming boob,

Simply not trying hard enough…yet trying just enough,

Unable to see that I am foolishly trying to follow dreams

That are nothing more than little lies that do nothing more

Than eat away at my heart & soul,

While I haphazardly…try & stay in control,

Playing it cool while allowing myself to continue

Writing, creating, wanting nothing greater than the chance to share…

When I should wake up and admit…that most people simply don't care

About the ups & downs of a singer/songwriter, writer, dreamer,

Unless they are given that chance of a lifetime to shine,

With many having more luck & fortune than mine, than most,

Being more talented, more well known, more hardworking…than I,

Less obscure,…with less adversity to face…than I…

& maybe there is sufficient equality amongst dreamers, movers & shakers,

With not enough attention, appreciation, open mindedness & time

For the mass of dreamers that we are…from our dear human race;

Please discover my beautifully awful music @ wrathbliss.com. Thank you!

We will & must…survive our struggles, while living, loving, laughing, creating, sharing,

Daring to dream, daring to live our lives OUR way, Curiously….

Appreciating & Thriving through each Chance & every Blessed Day-

SARCASTIC TEETH UPON MY NECK

("Why would I name this "Sarcastic Teeth", when I am mildly ashamed of having crooked, crowded teeth.
I should stay away from TEETH references in the future.. Geesh! LOL or not")

Suffering from these Dead Hair Questions and the Unfairness of it All,
Setting expectations too high could result in a greater fall,

Choices….

To climb that highest mountain or to fail within Failure's grand scheme,
With uncouth compromised commitment,
Wishing to feel accomplished while following such constipated dreams,
Feeling lost like a tiny forgotten old dead hair upon my maturing head,
Balanced in between shades of grey, brown, and ever aging red,
This human being that I be from head to toe, in mind, heart & soul,
Existing….
Beneath that bold sun beating down hot and bright with brilliant might,
Wrathfully wishing with well intent
That I may so have the opportunity to return to my zestful passionate self,
Full of Life, Meaning & essence on this given night-

Or…..
Pick it, pluck it, and take it away,
Like my hopes & dreams have been lost in the grindings of day to day,
As I notice those flaws upon me, & those flaws within,
Where my failures lead me, and how my failures never cease to end,
Right where my bitter warm confidence so happily dares to begin,
Where I want to keep it, up high, so that it will no longer
Care to fall apart & descend-

Stare I, at those reflections of a man, that man I am today,

Insecurely wishing, wanting more before my short time bleeds dry,

Before I myself betray myself chained between dismay & my loathing self,

Regurgitating tales of how I must live before I die, how I must try,

With abundant issues within me, depleting my such & such,

Like unseating deprivation to no longer deprive myself of sight & touch

While parlaying to my own self-deprecating nuances, once in a while,

So that I may conjure more determination than not, on certain days,

Quantized in terms of abundance, something like more than much,

At this very moment…before I cave in to that feeling of feeling

Overwhelmed & confused, my ego & my heart, so thoroughly bruised,

For no digital means will allow my imagination,

To go unshared, nor unused, nor unread, nor unheard, nor unknown-

For today, this hair upon my head, deeply dug within my scalp,

Has me begging for the answer to the question that I refuse to ask

Time & time again, complaining while crying foul, writer with no mask,

Ruthless traveler of rhyme & word with expression as my task,

Wear well I, this head of hair above this disguise of sarcasm,

Trying to figure out if each hair is in place, or if each hair displaced,

Like each moment of my life, analogous to a life beyond repair,

With heavy hope & heart in hand, as a child & as a man,

I dare to question,

"Why is Life so beautiful, and yet, so damningly unfair?"….

& so…very…TRAGICALLY…short

For the choice is mine, the choice is yours,

To talk, to dream, to spitefully abort,

Or to create, to share, to inspire….to LIVE,

Striking a thought while striking a chord,

No matter what outcome dear Life has to give;

Just Another Flawlistically Honest Pity-Fool at his Pity Party

Here they are…
In both words, verbs, vowels, consonants & more,
My imperfections wrapped up before you on these white pages,
Each word, each thought, like my heart upon my sleeve….
For all to read, for all to see,
My rise,
My fall,…

Sweet & sour, light & dark..& everything in between,
Or maybe…simply…nothing more than mere verbose exaggeration,
Or an intense offering of groundbreaking poetical expression,
Written with improvical flow & character, with thoughtful application-

Be it a bird, a book, a writer, a poem, a plane, a rock, a ball,
A waste of time or not, to be or not to be,
This work of heartfelt express art was written by the likes of me,
Containing contaminants of precious thoughts,
A gift of soul,…offered to a society that is saturated by day to day poets,
Offering such
Wildly gathered word equations that equate to what will easily be deemed
As no more than nothing at all,
Written by one that believes he consists of less splendor & more flaws,
Unseen, unheard, unknown as that nobody at his own pity party
That insists on abiding & writing by his own expressive laws;

And so I've heard…"Less is more"
Or….could more…simply…be …
The best way that I can express myself as ME!

The Compulsive Disorders within that Plague of Me

Something that might remind a curious nose of onion & garlic scents,
For at times, I wreak of disdain & a self-deprecative, insecure stench,
All in line, my body, heart and mind, together with each and every sense,
Sensing my way day by day, night by night,
Valuing my talents as no more than a buck & a fistful of common cents-

Admitting that me, myself & I, are a triple threat of optimistic based
Failures, plagued by my intense ways of
Believing in those little things like 'dreams and things',
Like a child suckling on the tit of dear sweet Lady Chance,
My wrongs keep me seductively induced in her stream of charming milk,
Romanced by the tasteful hope of what could be
If only it would be for me,
Finding myself in this farfetched dreamscape,
Knee keep in the groin of my imagination,
Whilst I suckle upon her bosom
Whilst trying to unlock the doorway to a better destiny,
Wanting, needing ..to be…more happy & more free,
With not an ounce of pain, regret…or guilt stirring within
Those many parts of myself & me-

I am to be enjoyed…for all of my many spoils,
My thoughts, my wrongs, my rights, my compulsive nature,
Raveled together like 4 combined seasons, blood, tears & soil,
Each one to be enjoyed and savored until you are satisfied & full,
For I consist of a furious love, imperfectly perfect, mostly undull,
While my heart whole heartedly plays in the breadline, sharing that
Symphony of my desires, awaiting my syncopated date of expiration,
Flowing freely, word by word, to and fro, befuddled with concentration,

So attached to my odd way of being, and my odder way of thinking,

Aloft, alas, side by side, hand in hand, chance uncompromised,

Disaster implemented like a wild card ghost, unannounced

On the brink of my own destruction,

Noticing the coils in that mattress of my reality,

Like a painting of the flaws in my design that crookedly hangs before me,

Feeling the dullness of that sharp knife that cuts through the fabric

Of my day while wincing through the pages of my fears, flaws & issues

Like a seeing eye dog leading its master to the light of forgiveness,

While I witness this storm of me, embracing that plague of me....

…..With each of my compulsive disorders lined up like ducks, all in a row,

like happy lil ducks walking into the face of callous shotgun wielding foes,

from my longest hairs to my shortest toes,

admitting those things I honestly still don't know,

as I learn daily that I am more than unsalted gravy

seeking my own internal seasonings out like a timekeeper seeks

a well wound watch unworn by the chaos that time can cause

for someone such as me, such as I,

reaching out for any reason to live my life,

without feeling likeI'm barely alive…just trying to survive,

my every flaw & all, my bleeding gums, crowded teeth & all,

whether I rise, ..or whether I fall,

for I understand that I may wreak of failure from time to time…
but this part time loser has gotten so much better
at making sweet apple pie out of apples before they die,
as it all begins with the will that you must have to purely try,
…once that pathetic, time wasting urge to do nothing subsides;

"I've wasted too much time getting here…This I do realize.
For that ..to you, and to myself, I do apologize."

Catching Certain Elements of Conspiracy by the Horns-

Wild like those swaying, crashing branches
That harshly impact us through that ruined system before us,
Drawing us closer to devastation's grand tree trunk
Pointing and leading us on like sheep to slaughter,
Herding us with advertive means,
Signs, Posters, Sex, Perfection,
Willing to raise our interest through
Such slight of hand perversion,
Hoping that we fall to their knees with an erection
To buy, to follow, to wrap our arms around them,
Opening up our wallets, our credit while dripping wet,
No matter our budget, our class,
The worst that can happen is addictions and high debts,
Concocting socially psychological pitfalls by way of tests,
As they figure out those many weakness' of our society,
Like cattle, like mice, like monkeys, like life being led
By the our senses, taste, sight, sound,
By our foolish desire to follow the piper up or down,
In fear, afraid, DREADFULLY dumbed down,

Allowing business to fill our lives with such fillers,
Poisons, toxins, unneeded abundances of sugars, fats and salts,
While they stack profits sky high in sky high vaults,
Surrounded by products that seem more like silent killers,
While we seep within whiskey wounds & pipe dreams,
Finding folded maps that we unfold in haste
Whilst trying to find our way, our treasure,
Growing wiser, older, uncovering Life, Love & its terrific schemes,
As we try and stay alive,

Or …as we give in …to our most inevitably endeavored End,

As we discover that Life was a choice, And Love was a feeling,

As we entered without a friend,

We will exit with no more time for answers,

Dying with so many unanswered questions in question,

And in time…Becoming forgotten,

And in time…Our remains, nothing but rotten,

As Time only preserves the Living,

As the Living will move on

While the Dead enter that pitch black new dawn;

I BATTLE I, ..Belly to Thigh, For my heart, my brain, my LIFE

In battle with those deep infested enemies of mine
Mutinously entrenched in the fields of my mind
Within the bergschrunds of my distant & foolishly followed Dreams,
Plotting against my passion & resiliency
In that precipitous, deep dark durable delicateness of myself,
Wishing to soon be rescued from those ill urges,
Wanting to be liberated from sugar, salt & fat cravings,
Including sleep apnea, stress, & those mild clouds that internally depress,
While falling apart over that lack of energy & weight gain,
Boldly searching for willpower, using these words to honestly confess
That behind these close quartered enemy lines,
I exist with tragic amounts of triglyceride bombs bursting in air,
Pondering just how that easily prescribed thyroid medication could be
Keeping me there, here, in between feeling better & worse,
Where nothing seems to be working, with sweet death I am flirting
Whilst eating healthier, being active, working out, trying,
Still dealing with my energy levels stalling all too often,
Marooning myself, feeling unfit, unhealthy, on the fast path to a coffin-

Damage already done, instilled with such flawed & purposeful potential,
Up against the wall with fear before me, reaching for my heart & soul,
Feeling as if I am slowly falling head first into a dark & cold foxhole....
While trying to shake free, break free from that weaker part of me,
Firing off rounds from my emotional gun of hopes & wishes
Of how I wish & hope to finally eat correctly, eating healthily,
While trying to get back my momentous momentum
Escaping from that place...where I feel so very,
Strained, stressed and sleepy,....

Wondering about all the damage done within my mainframe,

Trying to stay humanly sane,

While these & those assorted toxins continue to pollute me, doing me in,

Knowing that changing those old & dreadful bad habits have healed

What I once was, though I'm faltering still,

A self-made slave chained to that which slowly kills,

At times you'll find me on my knees, begging please...

For a happy pill, for a healthy key,

Wishing for a one way ticket away from the possibilities

Of cancer, diabetes & any other horrid disease-

Wanting to get my life back, to take my life back

Before I end up as just another statistical heart attack

On a temporary slab, a three stack rack,

All Caused by & due to my unhealthy eating habits,

Not because I was a user of meth, cocaine, heroin or crack....

So before I fall to that grand scale of dreadful dying

I will continue as I have, I will keep trying,

Trying again & again to get back up again after each failure,

Upon my feet again, striving to feel that feeling of intensity,

Once again..feeling & being healthy, alive, motivated, vibrant & free,

Wanting a much better, healthier outcome for me,

So that I may experience as much life as possible, while following dreams,

Enjoying each moment in time with my loving family,

Instead of being in a constant internal tug of war,

With 3 pounds lost, 10 pounds gained, living on seesaw on contempt,

I battling I,...until my end,

Fighting for my heart, mind, life, dreams & soul....once again;

BOMB BOUQUETS BURSTING across the skies of Denial

Within that dying life, under the rainbow, In the belly of the beast,
Living with that Demon of drink, viciously drowning your liver,
Suffering from such a severe state of self-imposed Alcoholism
As the bullet, the gun, & that cold ….out of control urge
To pull that loose & willing trigger;

Explosive scenarios toasting chaos with erect pinky salutations,
Enduring perverse travesty loads while introducing mouth to bottle top,
Bottle to mouth, liquor to liver, binge drinking to end the frustrations…
Wondering why there is a liquor store on every corner across our nation,
Meeting those abundant demands with swelling supply….

So many reasons to drink & drown, gulp & swallow,
All in the name of washing away the monotony, stress, grief & strife,
Drink after drink, stumbling, falling, passing out through life,
Nightly drinker, selfish thinker, drunken swagger, daily swigger,
That obsessive, compulsive, addictive… greedy liquor ni**er,
Taking your chances by living in such a dangerous manner,
Binging for release, a fumbling drunk,
Waking up in a numb state, detached, no longer able to fool, to flatter-
For without that next drink, it doth seem that nothing else matters…
But drinking down each bottle, out drinking the town,
Liquor as your water, liquor as your air,….
Addictions in the life of an addict are never fair,
But opening your eyes to your precious life
Might mean something to you and your family,
If only you could see past the vomit that blankets your ears & eyes,
Beneath all of the excuses & lies, there remains your beautiful Life;
PLEASE! Put down the bottle & Pick up your Life;

Art is a Peaceful Disaster in the Battlefield of your Heart

Waking up from slumber swollen with suggestive ideas,

Stressful dreams had me pulling, pushing, twisting

The nerves, hair & teeth of my subconscious

Wasting away from my worries,

In the eye of my passionate furies,

I know just what I'm missing,

This Catastrophe of me, myself and truly I,

Surviving single handedly beneath this grayest, darkest sky,

Doing my best to rest up for battle

That I will surely engage in that war of Me VS MYSELF & I,

Comprised of both...my worst enemy & my closest ally,

Knee deep in the trenches of World War MVMA (Me VS Me again),

Unveiling my issues, my flaws and insecurities with each written page,

Trying to succeed while separating my wants and needs,

Wishing someone could hear my pleads, watching you watching me…

Wondering when I'll finally get it right & grow from a seed into a tree…

Without me, myself and I caught up in such a grueling fight

Of my dark & light,

Treading carefully on that narrow ledge of reality,

Two steps from what could be a dirgeful drop into insanity,

Witnessing those voracious battles between the lazy me and the active me,

Until eventually…I internally cry myself to sleep

Seeking some sort of sane version of tranquility

On another confusing night, let down by myself & humanity…..

Hoping that…one day soon….I might finally get IT right!

I might finally get LIFE right!

By finally gettin' ME right!

No longer loathsomely battling from within,

No longer ensnared by my capricious ill melodies & written redundancies

There...

Beneath the grayest of skies, in the deepest, darkest seas of myself & me,

I wish to be more confident, stronger, fearless, in reason, in rhyme,

Focusing on the best of times,

Riding each storm out on the back of mighty tides...

Saved from the ongoing Wars Within,

Before I cave in, crumbling on all 4 sides,

Aiming onward for a more positive direction I shall keep

Before I end up 6 feet below where my Lover doth weep;

Crumbling on all 4 Sides with hints of Hope'n'Optimism VS Pessimism

Captivated by my appetite for writing round my own expressive
Tree of self-deprecating misery,
Like some form of self-loathing witchery,
Believing that if I could only release those negative parts of me,
Soon enough, out would flood my optimism, so ecstatically in abundancy,
And perhaps, just as ridiculously filled with my many trite redundancies-

Never the less,
Optimistically,
I shall….
Tread on,
Enduring the harshness of dusk
While appreciating that ever so,
Come & go…
Beauty of dawn,
Climbing mountains, taking leaps,
Living, dreaming, playing for keeps-

Falling down at times, slacking, feeling numb, motionless, lacklusterly lost,
Awaiting a new sense of urgency, a titillating thaw from the frost,
Something like an escape from the worst of me, my SELF & I,
With no award ceremony planned, I lay resting, wearing no suit'n'tie,
Grappling with the hoops & cantankerous red tape of my being,
Somewhere in between those many simplicities & complexities of me….

Wondering just how long I'll last before my passions return again,
As I acknowledge how awful I am at finding a flourishing friendship,
With so many difficulties that I've experience whilst trying to befriend
A friend, as this man I am, dashingly obscure, eccentric with no end….

More than once in a while…I feel that my dreams are worthless,
Like tiny slow sinking ships lost within an ostentatious & stirring sea,
Searching for some semblance of purpose while trying to persevere
Wreaked and rocked by ill choices and circumstances, future unclear,
That future that my Destiny doth vigilantly embrace
With ruefully reserved open arms, caught up in that crazy epitomic chase
Throwing myself under the bus of my wrongs in order to save face
Watching as my dreams wear thin, unable to find my place-

Beneath the grand sun of Reality's devastatingly hot charring rays,
I feel continuously burned to a standstill,
The evidence is great,..for I continue giving up, feeling overwhelmed,
This peasant pheasant with tainted hope and broken wings
Lost at sea somewhere in the in between of stingray stings,
Hard knocks, hard rocks, for I am averse to following unsavory flocks,
Found in the depths of a semi-treacherous society amongst other things,
Instead of on my secluded dark ship of unlived & decomposing dreams,
Taking full responsibility as the master of my downfalls & self-disaster,
Along with my failing, flailing self, spread out over my checkered history,
For on this day, back when, back then, no matter where, how or when
I still manage to continue on that pathetic path of foolish trends…
But tomorrow, once again, with redundant rapport
The Fallen me shall rise again, standing up with hope as my sword…

Trying once again,…with hope in heart, hand & throat,
This man, parent, pathological poet,
This pianist, this human being, still seeking some miraculous antidote
That could center me, for once & for all, before & after each rise & fall….

As more than a mere dreamer doing more or less than I can…

Existing as more than just some average diatribically diabolic good man…

No longer existing to battle within,

Finally free from my own bitter inner enemy…

My worst to my best, me, myself & I,

The hunter, the hunted, the truth, the lie,

Finding myself in the bloody thick of a passionate collision

Colluding with prideful conduct with my closest ally,

Doing what I can, acting and reacting,

Writing and believing, hopeful to venture onward,

Moving on, moving forward, day by day, word by word,

Being buoyantly able to forge on, new dawn to new dusk to new dawn,

Before the worst in me returns, set on committing mounds of wrongs…

Opening those freshly healed wounds from within again,

Blindly trapped between the beauty of romance & the tragedy of chaos,

Whilst I learn that Life & Love both arrive, hand'n'hand with pain & loss

No matter how many times I've find myself at war within

Wielding such brutal words of treachery and self-aimed deception,

I know that I no longer want to watch those walls crumble around me

Over & over again & again, repeat, replay, rewind….

With unpleasant disgust bubbling up within………..once again,

As my unanswered prayers, dreams & hopes deteriorate from within,

Lost in thoughts of how this nightmare in/of me, may never find an end-

For I must find a way to escape this mess,

A way to accept me, myself & I, heart on sleeve, soul on chest,

From my worst to my best,

And if such a pledge cannot be honored, I admittedly admonish that

In this inane maze of battle, it doth seem I will remain without refrain

Growing more insane day by day, excluded from where I could be,

With nothing more than those many foiled attempts behind me,

Friable & afraid of what comes next, feeling beneath the weather,

Trapped in the cortex of some witchy crafty hex,

Hanging, dangling from those partially fissured ego twigs, perplexed,

Confessing confidentially, page by page,

In & thru this book,

Declaring myself like some expressive vortex

Oh how I've become nothing more than polluted noxious air

Watching my dreams die like poisoned birds,

Crying like a baby in his very own crib of wrong turns & bad choices,

Going crazy from hearing only three convicted voices,

That of..Me, Myself and I,

Wishing for a pardon from this dreary sentence of life….

While those inner convicts of my Heart, Mind & Soul

Wish that I could overpower the darkness of my fermenting undertow…

That which brings me down, that negative energy within me,

That darkness within that has pledged to bring me down redundantly,

Crashing to the ground,

As the best of me recovers me, myself & I, along with my dignity…

As WE gather hopeful and hopelessly with a heaping spoonful of humility

To once again get back our life, my destiny, and our combined humanity,

While those gross amounts of Dark and Light battle it out in our Society...

+We march, we walk, we pray, we talk, we strive, we unite, we fight

For Peace, Equality, Our Present & Our Future, Ourselves, Our children

With words, with wisdom, with understanding…instead of violence+

While Good & Evil rotate from East to West, North to South,

As do the rest, I continue to battle it out within my stalwarty SELF….

Hoping that soon,…today, I will finally arrive

At the end of another colorless rainbow over heart, mind, and soul,

Where I may finally find that colorfully pleasant place away

From those rabidly reoccurring undertows-

Through this & that, I've continued to learn that no matter what WE try,

We can't escape the way it is, the way we live our lives…

As reality reinvents itself like some syndicated TV Show,

For what we are internally, is the best of friends, the best of foes…

And no end shall come of this with the twinkle of a star

Nor the wiggle of a nose,

No matter how pathetically pungent the day,

No matter how sweetly scented the rose,

The possibilities of change only happen to those

That are not afraid to admit that wrong paths & ideas were chose,

And though the battle in between skin and soul continue on,

One day sooner than the next, my greater good will rule my dawn;

(If there is something you want to do….give it a try.

Don't be afraid of failing.

Be afraid of missing out on an opportunity

To experience something new & wonderful about yourself & life;)

I do more than suppose that she is my IRISH ROSE

Under & Overwhelmed…misunderstood & safely sheltered…be I,

Where she keepith me warm & safe from edgy elements out there, in hell,
She can't keepith me safe from my own chaos in here, wherest I dwell-
She raises me up after those many indubitable bouts between myself & I,
But she can't understand my every weakness, my every fear,
Though she endures this journey beside me,
At times, I am a maddening most frustration causing burden of a man,
And at times, I am to her, a dream man, her dream man-
At times, a certain disaster of a man, with no hope, no bread, no bacon,
Watching me flail around, I know that she seeith me to be at times
Like a dissident fish out of boiling water, with no direction, with no plan,
And if there is a plan, how surely easy it is for me to lose focus at times,
More than I'd care to admit. So, I do continue on with life, with dreams,
Through my good days, warped, worn and dried out days as well-
On those days that have me throwing in the towel, losing to hell
Haste-fully retreating back to that shelter where I feel mostly safe,
Back in her arms, her warmth, her love, her embrace,
By my side, my loving conduit of support & grace,
Together….Braver,
Standing shoulder to shoulder with my lover, with my savior-

As long as it might last, we stand, believing that it just might
Enduring our trials & tribulations, each chapter, each fight
Before that next war within myself, I & me is cast,
Doing my best to conjure up ways to overcome my past,

52

Reaching through the wiry branches of my confidence
Straight down to the core of my conscience,
Back when I was a child saluting another form of turmoil,
Figuring out just how contaminated I am today....
Because of where I come from, from where I began,
Born a baby, baby to teen, teen to man,
Wanting to fly like an eagle with no clue how to land,
Wishing I had followed a less narrow path, had a better plan-

Seeing how crippled my fate was from the start,
Acknowledging how I ever became this man with
Tainted ego, bruised confidence, this hopeful hopeless tainted heart,
For if I could find a way to fix this mechanism of me,
I would gladly take myself apart piece by piece, part by part,
Year by year, and fix myself, from my end to where it was I so did start
To go so wrong, so off course, so off track, splintered & off center,
So that I could start again, and accomplish my dreams
With more and more productive passionate steam;

One fish of Hope in a river of quandaries

Walking on a log, spilling down a stream,
Could things be any worse than they seem,
Waking up confused, with dreams so scattered, unlived and bruised,
Hope is a drink that goes down best with belief,
Loneliness is stubborn, stealthy like a midnight thief,
And no matter what, T r y i n g…is how I spell relief,
Getting back on that electric bull again,
Be the ride long, be the ride brief, knowing that I'm alone in this,
Another chance at living, making dreams come true, I shall not resist……

So short on time we are, & I am even shorter on friends by far,
Stumbling through this maze of me & these draining daylight scenarios,
For where I end up, is where I'll be,…. I do suppose,
With my daughter growing from my baby girl to my baby teen,
Seeing how distance once again meets us at in between,
While I am closely entwined with my Baby Boy and my lovely Irish Rose,
Hopeful I am to resolve my many quandaries to lessen my troubled woes,
Striving for a better future while decreasing my current stress load,
As I continue to make my way down dauntingly haunting… dimly lit paths,
Still growing, learning, churning passion within my swollen heart & soul,
Living out my destiny, dream by dream, fight by fight,
Staring in the mirror, looking past my aging wrinkles while in midflight-
Hoping, wishing, praying, …whispering to myself…
"It'll be alright".....It will be alright,
I will be alright, we will be alright
Tomorrow may still be a blurry question mark, distant & unclear,
But today we'll be alright, for we have love & hope on our side….
And today, I'll will try my best to cease this war between Me, Myself & I,
So that I may finally escape those bold steel bindings of my complexities,

To share with you something true and sweet,

Where happiness, joy and fun doth meet…

Here, where from that battle between me, myself & I, I shall retreat…

And to you..I promise…that I will get through this chapter for us,

And to you..I offer many Thanks and Appreciative sincerities,

For enduring the crashing waves of my crisis filled circumstances,

And …for staying beside me, sharing your life, your smile, your laughter;

Breaching the stubbornness of my Dome,

Because with YOU,

Because of YOU,

My son Finn, my love O, my daughter D…, I am not Alone-

I'm getting there,

I'm getting somewhere..

I'm getting closer..

I'm getting warmer,

No longer a fleeing heartbreak sympathizer with a fatalistic spirit,

I am charmed by foolishness no more,

No longer willing to sulk in the reflection of my failures,

Finally free from that dark tomb of snakes beneath me…

I'm reaching out through expression,

This fabulous way of creative suggestion,

Ending my cerebral congestion,

Expelling feelings and thoughts word by word,

Imperfectly displaying my wicked written ways

I'm breaking the rules, not abiding by what is known as the norm,

Extending my heart and soul, page by page,

Releasing my insecurities,

Those that have been drenched in darkness of my disappointments,

Peeling off that heavy dark shell, word by word,

Saving myself from this inner battle, this inner rage,
As I've been so displeased with myself at least half of the time,
But ..what splendid wonders can be found in expressing through rhyme,
Rhyming down those internal brilliant avenues of my heart and mind,
While extracting such sweltering words from my soul,
Speaking with, expressing, leaping bounds with my hands,
Forgetting about our diversely timorous society
And its tremendous, prodigious expectational demands-

Remembering that I am no God, nothing special,
Just a conspicuous dreamer, just a man,
A loving father, a loving son, blood, skin & bone,
Imperfectly formed from head to hand,
Perfectly aware of my flaws, internal and external,
Vulnerable and beyond, (so please discover me before I am gone)
..As I'm aware that I'm none the less
Filled to the brim with such wonderful pros, and such pathetic cons,
Wanting to achieve what is right…though I may be doing it all wrong,
Never the less, this is my book…where my words do so belong;

"Once, I was a man trapped in my own dark,
self-deprecative arena, surrounded by crowds of self-pity,
At battle, at war…trying to even up the score,
Seeking the right path, the right door,
Like a floundering out of water fish….
Finally realizing that the battle has been between
Me, Myself & I & my Failures & Foolishness"-

56

The WRITER & the READER

Here I brood, the man, the poet, the author, within these many pages
So that YOU the Reader may feel my many colorful stages,
My many flaws, insecurities, my beauty to my internalized mellow rages,
Freeing myself with words & rhyme from those cold steel cages,
Breaking the rules of poetry, becoming the worst poet of the ages-

Choices of expressive inner voices a writer doth have,
To fill such pages with imagination or reality, from hate to love,
To fill such pages with those steamy details,
From the darkness of demons to the saving grace of those Angels above,
Writing what so many will read up until their eyes can no longer read on,
With shared feelings that will have you in tears by dusk,
Or feeling so very rather orgasmically accomplished by dawn-

From ROMANTICAL fantasies to brave displays of heroic passion
To saucy sweet erotica incantations that wrap your cerebral thighs around
Such sticky sensuality stimulators that drip with sex, lust and sweat
As readers compare and contrast their lives with those pages before them,
Wondering if they'll ever live out such a story, such a lover, such a friend,
Reading pages that drive them to continue on through the night,
Blindly into Desire's warm erect lair of fascination, so juicy and wet,
Immersed in those plenteous pages, their own mundaneness forgotten
Thanks to Authors that use such scintillating chains of words that flatter
Describing bodies & actions in such a deliciously descriptive manner,
From a single businessman that generously rams his secretary steadily
With his hungry, passionate and most willing erected manual capabilities,
To evil dragons being slayed whilst knights & maidens beith getting laid-

Where a Prince can meet his Princess
In the company of rabbits, birds and bees,
Making mad love to her in the warm summer breeze
Beneath magical willow trees,
Where a woman can be ravaged by
A complicated man always willing to give her what she wants & needs,
Fulfilling her fiery desires in more ways than one,
With swelled & hardened ardent tenacity-

For she seekith a man spread across a number of pages
That would be so very incapable of any sort of fervid depraving
While outdoing those real-life men that lack the
Drive, stamina…& the time required to feed her carnal cravings,
Sadly, unable to offer up as many succulent moments
That she would prefer,
That she most surely deserves-

So, Thank God for those Authors that fill the pages of those books
That keep us wetly dreaming, yearning & living with hope,
Through fantasy, allowing readers to romanticize & self-grope,
Allowing us to keep on keeping on, allowing us to cope,….
Moving on, writers, readers, people like YOU, me, him & her,
For I know that I am the only man, author, poet, dreamer, lover
Over any other, on or off page, that my true Love doth prefer;

And maybe one day we'll do more than just live through pages
That bring us love, lust and ecstasy, romance and tragedy,
On pages that divide us…or keep us together within our modest reality,
Delivering such surreal scenarios from real life to fantastical epic fantasy,
So that we might one day know that the pages of our own lives were
Just as compelling, heated, passionate, rewarding & meaningful, undull,

As those many pages read, as those many pages turned

From books bought, books borrowed, used and new,

And those many yet to be discovered books

That gather dust on a lonely shelf,

As would my book, if it were not for YOU,

For I have been awaiting your sweet arrival,

Wishing to be read by your beautiful eyes,

Opened up by your soft hands,

Discovered by your mind & heart,

Able to see your smile,

As YOU continue to search for that one perfectly imperfect moving story

To immerse YOUR deepest self;

IF It BE A Case by Case by case by case scenario

The Deaf may not hear it, The Blind may not see it,
But those with heart upon sleeve will surely feel it,
The busy may not make time, The lazy may not take time,
But those few that do, will surely possess an open mind,
For it is all a case of case by case scenarios-
With outcomes that are best described as Unexpected & Unknown,
Ranging from children to adults that are wise & full grown,
Depending on so many varied statistical ratio studies & factors,
A case by case scenario of whether or not what one expresses
Will truly trend or not is what seems to only seem to matter…..
Giving our utmost attentive disposition to that which merely flatters
If it be..
What is shared by sight and sound does spread through epic chatter,
If what is shared is good enough for sailing on that viral attention wave,
If what is deemed as worth your time peaks your interest quickly,
As that case by case scenario becomes a brainwashing mechanism,
Some escape, some give in, trapped between dumb downing schemes…

And perhaps…this is all I have to offer that suffering world,
Parts of this artistic, emotional man that I am…
Feeling hopeful…..while feeling damned….

And though The Deaf may not hear it,
And though The Blind may not see it,
And though The Reader may not read it,
I will continue to Express and Write IT;

WHETHER OR NOT YOU APPROVE IT OR DISLIKE IT---.--.---
As should YOU, as should WE, feel it…express it, create it, share IT;

A bird, not an anchor......

A bad day can have you feeling like a huge steel

Mega burdensome anchor-

Weighing you down like an immobile ship lost at sea,

With a widespread array of frustration hovering over your hull;

Good thing you're not a ship.

So don't let a bad day weigh you down like that.

Spread your wings and know that tomorrow you can fly once again-

Attached to nothing but passion, love, desire, dreams & possible sins,

Free like a bird, not weighed down like some slowly sinking rusty anchor;

Brain Salad Worrisome Cerebral Flurries

The Tools of Technology have no keys to unlock our destiny

While the blind lead the blind through wrathful tragedies

Wandering through time hoping for change,

Wondering if bliss will ever wrap its lips around us

To suck out the venom that thrives within us,

That violence and angst within us

That ignorance that continues to divide us,

That death merchant that perilously taints us

As technology takes us to so many places,...

Escapism is our main mission,

Still unable to undo that chaos that sadly rages

Lead around like cerebral puppets on wireless leashes

Manipulated by those puppet masters that cloth & feed us,

Fattening us up to feed on us like vampirical leeches....

Their dark & tainted ignorance tends to stand taller than

What those few good people have tried to teach us

Through the pages of time and books

We still can't embrace that which is most important of all

That which saves us from the hooks

Of a dumbed down existence where we hang, where we fall,

While the few that know the truth and have the

Power of such grand design, such grand control,

Controlling those many pretty lights & colorful signs,

In order to one day control our feverish hearts & gullible minds,

Keeping us blind & detuned in their production lines

Offering our bits & pieces...new life, like a modern Dr. Frankenstein..

Those flocks of us that gather like nothing else could matter
But bigger, better brands that lead us by our eyes, our head, our hand
The more we think we need, the more we surely want,
As wizards with wands shaped like penis' acting like cunts
Manipulating & creating the fate of woman, child and man…
Throughout our home, throughout our land,
Addicting us to mass consumption is their business plan-

Floating like those poisoned fish that soon become our tasty dish
Lead around like willing mice with anything that fulfills our weakest vice
While some are more focused on raping every resource from the Earth,
Reaping, gaining, adding, growing, holding treasures, riches,
Wanting to experience life with the most unparalleled wealth
In the midst of corrupting our world and the core of our society
Never mind our health, offering such pretty packaged
Toxic poisons that cause such violent varieties of illness,
Hooking us due to our ignorance, weakness, our inert willingness-

Like those manmade preservatives & artificial
Chemicals that lengthen shelf life by months and years
As we no longer worry about our food spoiling a week from now,
WE still can't escape the mouth of fear
Eating, drinking that which self-destructs us internally,
With sickness & disease right between our ears,
Absorbing doses of evil, strain by strain,
We the frail, so fragile, so easy to manipulate & train,
Manipulated greatly by that dark force with avariciously ill intentions,
With a great unstoppable and corruptible momentous finger
Like some black scorpion in our bed, with a triple loaded stinger-

Pinpointing our flaws, wants and needs,
They have us groveling on our knees,
While our human imperfections have us trapped in such
A colorful rotating redundant bubble of deception-
Where all it takes is something within us
2 be altered somehow, some way,
LIKE those
Genetically Modified Foods, available around world, around the clock,
Available in brightly lit stores where they are always fully stocked,
They produce Genetically Modified Foods & Seeds of many varieties
LIKE they are
Somehow trying to Genetically Modify our consumption based Society-

Skewing our views & taste buds too,
Including our sense of reality & our rationality,
Our empathy, our lives, our world, our day,
No longer able to differentiate between right and wrong,
Life and death, worst and best,
When words no longer matter, where bullets
Chase bodies & heads, knives penetrate skin & chest,
That day our world becomes the home to such
Widespread brutal violence,
& OUR precious Peace, Love, Respect, Humanity & Understanding
Are forever silenced-

Which could surely happen if we continue to be
Lead on wireless leashes like happy blind puppets
Playing along, manipulated by products, power, greed,
Wet dream dazes and bright shiny glittery things,
Allowing ourselves to be educated & fed through
Those same tainted tubes that infect us daily

That weaken our abilities to think, change.. & grow
Controlling what we want & need, believe & see,
What we think is right & wrong, & what we think we know,
As we imagine ourselves sailing
Out and about on such a beautiful sunny day,
The reality is, we are tragically sinking,
Swept away in the sweet & sour lies of our own demise,
Within a most entrancing, misleading,
All consuming, mind numbing undertow of disgust,
That is the future that they are creating for us;

It's Only a Word...unless....It is more than a Word

((F-BOMB ALERT/WARNING: Explicative Language!!!))
Rated- Frack'n R!!!!!!! NOT for Children under 18.
PLEASE Stop READING NOW if you are easily offended!!

Is FUCK just a Word, unless it is a state of Mind....?

Double standard or not,

Fuck...is only a word, unless it is your state of mind,

Fuck...is only a word, unless it is your way of life,

Fuck...is only a word, unless it is your way of thinking,

Fuck...is only a word, unless it is filled with ill intentions,

What a fucking fuck of a fuck this day has been,

If the word FUCK is used, you judge me while happily pondering

That I must be a filthy mouthed sinner spewing words of sin,

What a fucking fuck load of bad luck I'm having,

And if the word FUCK is used, you judge me while thinking

That I'm absurdly engaging in such vulgar based babbling,

It is only a word unless it's said with hate,

It is only a word unless it hurts someone,

It is only a word unless it starts a war,

It is only a word unless it evens the score,

Fuck...is only four letters long,

A word used in life, in love, in movie, in song,

Fuck...is spelled F followed by U, C and K,

Fuck can describe a feeling of simply getting laid;

Hands that express through cartoons, paintings, movies & words…
Could very well be used to show disrespect
To a culture, a religion, a race…
But a GUN, a hand on the trigger,
Firing heated bullets at those you hate….
Is expression from a much darker, definite evil place----
A tragic sign of what was..
And what is still becoming of our declining human race---

A verb, a noun and idiom, a word none the less…..
Anger, vulgarity, pain, hate, evil, darkness,
Come from within us, residing within us,
Controlled by us, steered by us, decided by us,
Depending on our feelings, beliefs and choices,
And just how we aim to express ourselves,
While communicating with objects, actions & voices,
Instigating, manipulating, conspiring to harm those in your midst,
Allowing words to be used as weapons,
Acting out without thinking,
Driving after an evening of binge drinking,
Loading guns for a planned future massacre,
Apathetically strapping on bombs to make an explosive statement ….

one

two…

READY, SET

FUHBOOOOOOOOOOOOOOOOMMMmmmmmmmmmmmmm!
(explosive sound)

While there are some that exist daily…angrily, violently, hatefully reacting,

Yelling!!!, Screaming!!!..at the top of THEIR lungs, "FUCK YOU!!!"

And those victims in direct earshot perhaps think that THEY deserved it,

Your rageful fit, though we admit

That tone doth hurt more than those chosen heard words at times….

Further admitting… that actions doth hurt more than the words,

As words can hurt, they don't leave us bleeding out & dying in the dirt,

& though some words may hurt more

Depending on whom & how they are used,

Words don't leave your body black & blue,

They don't burn your skin or stain your sheets,

Though words have been known to end heart beats,

The way that certain words were said,

Has made people wish they were dead;

A word, an object, a thing, a saying,

Used for fun with the intent of playing,

Used to cause hurt and pain through hateful relaying,

Used by choice as a weapon, as a voice….

A bomb, a gun, a bullet, a hammer, a car, a knife,

A poison, a disease, a hateful thought, a hateful plan…

Anything can be used to harm or end the life

Of a woman, child or man,

If such a method of madness is continually chose,

If such a program of violence is regularly ran,

If empathy and the value of life continue to erode,

Hate & evil, through words, objects & actions,

Will continue to be found, through silence and sound,

Ignorance will travel achieving leaps and bounds;

So…perhaps expressive excuses do arrive a dozen at a time,

As should the reasons we have to think, feel & express

With heart, soul and mind,
With eyes open while we gain as much
Knowledge as we can to escape that which has us blind
With extreme prejudice and deep dark intent,
Utilizing words to show affection, love,
Words that tear a heart apart, Words that forever mend

Words used
To express, to describe, to share, to vent,
To break, to mend, to defend, to offend,
Our use of words really has no end,…

Words can hurt, depending on how they are used & said,
Words can start wars and moments of dread,
Words can open doors, or close doors instead,
Words open and close the possibilities of discussion,
Words turn us off and on, expressing love or lust instead,
Words cause everything from happiness to sorrow,
Words tell us of our past, today and tomorrow,
Words explain, words mislead
Words ask and answer questions,
Words are surely our primal obsession,
Words are the reason for our transgressions-

Some Words carry truth, Some Words carry lies,
& though words may hurt at times, Bullets through flesh… end lives;
It's only a word…unless it's your state of mind,

It's only a word…unless you mean to be that blind, as bat, as owl,

It's only a word…unless you emit evil within each consonant & vowel,

It's only a word…unless you wish to cause chaos and tragedy

It is only a WORD, it is only an object

Unless your state of mind is…."Fuck humanity",

With a weapon in your hand, screaming…

"Fuck your religion, Fuck your race, Fuck your life"……

In that case, if you so do believe that you are one of those

That enjoy using Words & Bullets to spread violence, hate, terror, pain…

Then please do work on yourself & your insecurities…

So that you can rejoin humanity & make a better World

For All, each man, woman, boy & girl

Instead of a horrid world where ignorant people

Feel the need to stand so foolishly Fucking TALL

While making everyone else feel so FUCKING small,

For this World, OUR WORLD is not for only YOU,

Our World is for One & ALL,

No matter OUR differences, size, shape, class, belief, religion,

WE are ALL Human Beings that deserve respect

And the chance to experience life, love…and dreams

Valuing life, knowing the difference between bullets & words,

Understanding that taking a life in the name of vengeance, is truly absurd;

Love doesn't require bullets. Peace doesn't require explosives.

Stop the RADICALS of EXTREME TERROR, with LOVE not Hate...

Words, Cartoons, Freedom, People, Unity, Difference....YOU FEAR!!!!

But DEATH you do not!! Becoming a martyr is the be all, end all?

Killing in the name of prophets, gods, money, personal beliefs,

Robbing & stealing lives like cowardly murderous thieves...

With evil intentions, existing & acting with such contradictive intentions,

Out on a mission to teach the infidels a lesson or a few,

With nothing more than Hatred as an offering from the likes of you,

As you hide behind religion, demanding respect,

Killing Charlie in the name of YOUR evil-righteousness...

For all that dreadful...tragic act did was ignite Our World in utter disgust,

For we aren't afraid of you and your terror spreading regime,

We aim to unite, we aim to fight against evil

Because we are free to believe what we will, say what we think & feel

Without the FEAR of someone like you targeting us for the kill

Because you don't like our words, our drawings, our way of life...

And one way...or another...

White, Black, Muslim, Christian, Jew, Palestinian, Iraqi, Russian & etc...

Each man, each woman, each human, will finally get IT..

That WE ARE FAMILY, that we are sister, that we are brother,

And though Freedom of Speech is darling...used for bad or good,

We shouldn't use it to satirically,...nor sarcastically,

Disrespect, disregard, divide...or offend, or kill each other over;

THEY Search for another World.....but what about OUR WORLD?

There they go again,
Spending millions & billions
On intergalactic travel plans,
To find a new home for the wealthier better man-

Deep space dreaming, deep space diving
Across the Universe in search of a new home
Where those that can afford to live
Will soon be living & thriving
Leaving the lower class behind
To live in a future muddle, barely surviving-

Fast forward dreamers dreaming
Searching for other life, for other planets
That they fantasize of calling home,
Where other life forms might be found,
Forgetting about the life on our Earth
That is beautiful & profound
Though taken for granted,
Though taken advantage of,
With more chaos shared than sharing love-

Continue on they will, they do
Never minding the likes of me & you,
Seeking something superior, fresh & new...
Where life could very well
Most certainly be sustained for a fortunate wealthy few,

Somewhere out there in that great big Universe,

Where only the wealthy & the powerful could possibly

Be the only ones to gain,

While the less fortunate remain,

And after all those years of mistreating her,

OUR planet continues to slowly die,

And for those of us that continue to try,

Against companies & chemicals & bigger dollar signs,

Once they find their new planet to call home,

With ships that carry them away,

Those that remain will at least not die alone-

Yes…those merry men looking for a place to start all over again,

Those starry eyed new planet seekers

With million dollar supporters…

Seeking a new planet to build their

Big & sprawling buildings & living quarters-

Voyaging through the stars for that new unknown Home

While we exist, survive, live…still watching, still allowing…such

Massive lethal pollution & waste to constantly consume our own,

Permitting people to propagate contaminants while growing richer

Those poisons that detrimentally decompose our air, water, soil, our lives,

While repeatedly raping, stripping, taking, using precious Mother Earth's

Every possible resource available in our here and now…….

No matter the price, no matter what or how

Elevated the warnings signs & significant dangers become,

More attention & finances are spent on space exploration

Than on our own current most essential priceless world & population,

Each person, each city, each nation….

So, when you have the funding for reaching out across the universe
With such a grand hunger, with such a deep thirst,
It must be easier to dream & seek out the unknown,
Leaving behind what you know for all those bright & new possibilities
Amongst those planets & stars
Instead of expending care & respect to that which is our responsibility-

For there is so much more that we could be doing to improve our home,
As we strive & struggle to change our ways day by day,
Those changes that are up to me & you to follow through,
So that our society may continue evolving & dreaming,
Showing love, understanding & respect to each other,
Knowing the value of life & love, good health & birth,
And the importance of our most precious, one and only
Most priceless planet..OUR dear, precious planet... Mother Earth;

For if Earth was really our Mother that bestowed to us
A place to live, to spend our lives...
Would we, would you... continue to treat & mistreat her so horribly?

And...if you believe that GOD created our planet,
As perhaps some..temporary gift,
Along with Our universe....
Would you leave it broken, spoiled, dying,
People divided, resources all used up, cloaked in terror & crime,
While you and your abundant bankroll & superior technology
Gallivant off through the stars...
Expecting to move to some other planet that be outlying,
After you've demolished this great gift of Earth?

So, while we strive to dream as natural explorers tend to do,

Searching the stars for another inhabitable planet,

By day, by night, out to discover a planet that is just right,

Which is of course…each human's right….

Let us not forget about our current planet, our current home,

Our People, Our Families, Our Neighbors, Our Future,

Before you exist Earth for some other planet….

I hope you fix the wrongs that you helped create

Before you call another planet your new destination,

Before you do the same as you've done with our world, with our society,

Letting it become so corrupt, poisoned, divided,

Before you leave it here to die,

Please do give repairing IT, another worthy try;

And we…should be ashamed…if we are seeking intelligent life out there,

Wanting them to notice us, to visit us,

To fulfill our fantasies,

Maybe even…answering all of our unanswered questions,

….ARE WE ALONE? Is there ANYBODY, ANYTHING, ANY LIFE

Out there….somewhere…some place in that wide open

Deep & dimly lit Universe of time & space….

Sure…why not!...

But…let us remember…Our Own Human Race & Our Planetary place;

Dear Sweet Children of Mine... The World.....

Dear DeLanna & Finn,

Our World is beautiful,
And though it may offer up some
Natural calamities & manmade chaos from time to time,
Never forget...That Our World is Beautiful...& so are YOU;

And though it may be our home, Our home away from home,
Our home in place of home,
Our World is beautiful,
And though it may seem too quiet or too dull,
Our World is beautiful;

Our World, our planet, our home,
Our round sphere, our globe, our circle in the universe,
Our dot in the equation of infinity,
Our heaven, our nest, our reality,
That splendid home to all humanity,
Where each woman, child & man deserves
To be treated with respect, kindness & equality,
Where each man, woman & child deserves
To know happiness, love, understanding, mercy and sovereignty-

Here, where we are one family, that of humanity,
Even though we may have different visions, beliefs,
We also share such important commonalities-

Be safe & well on your journey,
Enjoy each moment of your 'Life Experience'

While you age, discover, create, inspire, learn & grow,

Discovering romance, relationships, friends, & the strength of Love,

Taking it all in, the trees, the rivers, flowers, mountains, & heaven above-

For everything between Heaven above & Hell below

Can be discovered & found between sky & ground

Nightmares & dreams, hard work & indolence,

Love & hate, war & peace, necessity & indulgence,

Right & wrong, poem & song, living & dying,

Leading & following, Giving up & trying, Honesty & lying-

And though we have our differences, our differences should not divide us,

Like cold & hot, black & white, red & green,

Poverty & wealth, attraction & repulsion,

Repressing & expressing, boring & inspiring,…

While growing up in this beautiful World you will experience this & that,

Doing your best with your chin up through adversity,

Knowing that evil exists no matter how brightly the sun may shine-

Always believe in yourself, be that a challenge at times,

March on, following your dreams & heart with body, soul & mind,

For no matter how swiftly, strong & dark a storm may arrive or appear,

There is great beauty to be found, experienced & shared in our World,

In our lives, in our dreams, each minute, each day, each year

Appreciating, valuing…life, love, time, family & friends until the end,

Knowing the difference between Hopefulness & Hopelessness,

Assurance versus Fear, Words & Art versus Bullets & Guns,

For there is so much more about our World & this Life

That I hope to share with you during our time my Dear daughter & son;

Sincerely, With Love, Your Father T.D.M,

Blessed I am that you are here sharing this Life Experience with me-

The Timeless Appeal of Belief

Believe in a God,

Believe in a Devil,

Believe in something

Or nothing at all,

Believe in Good,

Believe in Evil,

That one shall rise,

That one shall fall,

Or you may choose to

Believe in nothing at all-

Believe in the Right,

Believe in the Wrong,

Believe that being meek

Is far better than being strong-

Believe it is fantasy, believe it is real,

No matter what you believe in.......

Believing in something, believing in nothing,

Does rather seem to have a certain timeless appeal;

The Poetically Gifted or The Poetically Cursed

To rhyme or not to rhyme,
To write or not to write,
To share your darkness,
To share your light-

To express or not to express,
To expel with raw conviction
Those emotions & thoughts buried well within
The depths of your closest enemy, your closest friend,
Sharing yourself verbally or in written word
With words that can allow one to feel nothing at all or so much more,
Deeming you as a unique & righteous poet
Or merely some crazy, rambling, writing, babbling, expressive whore,
Purging expressive offerings that are imbibed from heart & mind
To bear with honesty, to share, to inspire, raw & unrefined,
Without worrying about how those few readers might judge you
Based on how you think & what you've shared & written.......

That which might leave some removed, with a few possibly smitten
By skimming, by reading through your words of mild modesty
Uncompressed & combined with elements of your flaws & beauty,
The natural flowing, dreaming Poetical You
Pouring yourself out in a Panic of Prose,
Pleasing or displeasing, imperfectly sour & sweet to the bite
With words that lunge forth feeding a few frivolous bookworm appetites
While ranting & raving within the portals of rhyme & time
Like a fool would ever care to believe or be himself deceived
To think that being a poet these days would even matter at all...

Certainly....there are more than enough poets to cushion the fall
For those that seek to read line by line of words that rhyme
Instead of those more delicious & enticing fictional stories & such,
Those best sellers & favorites that sell for three times as much,
That do so delightfully take readers on grand journeys to & fro
Through well spun tales of heroes & foes,
Antagonists VS Protagonists, battling for power or romance,
While poetry & prose have become nothing more than
A super saturated, insignificant & most common
Excessively habitual & trite manner of verbal & written expression;

I get it. I admit it. There doesn't seem to be anything special these days
About being a poetically communicative person with such poetic ways-

That poetic person, like you, like me,
That enjoys sharing him/herself in many a prolific poetic verse
For there are so many poets and poems, ramblers of rhyme
That you may choose from, if poetry is what you hunger, what you thirst-

And as that Poet, I feel less unique, far less gifted, & extremely cursed,
Because my poetry is perhaps nothing more than garbled thoughts indeed,
For I know & understand that what I offer, my strengths & insecurities,
Have no grand audience hungering & thirsting for pages written by me,
Filled with my poetic stylings, my rambling ways of writing,
My wordsmithy manner of expressive demeanor,
Somewhere in between fatalistic, inviting & enlightening-

My rants, my stream of thought, my flow, my way with rhyme,
My run-on sentences filled with feelings, feeling more like wasted time
On pages of words, commas & dots, until maybe one day, I suppose,
When these or those words of mine will mean something more than prose
To someone other than me, feeling my words are more than mere poetry,
Once I am long gone & forgotten, my body parts far beyond rotten,
Resting upon one crowded dusty shelf will remain a part of my self
My heart, soul & mind, my most peculiar poetic syntactic flaws & all,
Being the evidence of my eccentric poetic endeavors, the rise & the fall;

The best Luxury in Life is....

Licking lamentive liquid laser lamps unluckily loathing little lazy lumps
waging wicked wonderful wasted wars experiencing explicative excursions
in intoxicating icy isolation driving devilishly deadly dangerous devices
feverishly favored frantic failures shameful sins seizing sunlight
conceived convictional complications
endless eager electric egocentric Elations
pushing pulling postponing preventing
magnifying my matchless mellow meager means
undertaking undeniable under-goings
becoming blistered buried beneath
tangled tangents that twist
turning terrible thoughts to
fantastic free fabricated fragments
of obvious optimistic
souls surely surviving
alive & attached, appreciating the ability to
LOVE, ...LIFE's true most precious luxury,
To Love,
To Be Loved;

Ra, Ra, Shish Boom Blah

Pouring in the cement, right on top of me, myself & I,
This, my foolish attempt at burying this foolish guy,
with that same cold cement running through my very veins,
That same cold cement I count on to keep me strong,
cold enough not break under the weight of everyday frustrations-
Yet, allowing me to remain warm enough to be me, passionately alive,
functioning as loving man, father, the unknown artist I am internally…

This open casket of my mind, birthing dreams that keep me insightful
and ready for another day of life to be shared, to be lived-
And for that opportunity & experience…
I'll gladly sign the dotted line, hopeful that today will have me
feeling rather liquidly prolific, rather splendid & cohesively centered.…
for as of yesterday,
I may have been feeling so very worn, & detrimentally descended,
yes, I may have felt like bailing out, giving way, breaking, caving,
when finally, my inner weakness found ways to be rescinded,
& with optimistic fibers I think, "Suicide is never right"…
linking that entire chain of me, with dark thoughts & doubts,
within that strong circle of I, within my inner Eye,.…

seeing, feeling, reeling, recomposing, breathing,
longing to achieve my goals & dreams,
escaping the cold callous grips of deception & fear
by reaching deep within myself, believing in myself.…
while that cold cement seems to be burying me with my own grief,
stealing my precious time like an uncommon thief,
for rest I need, in dear dire need of recharging for that new tomorrow
hearing whispers from within while I sleep, taking that slight gamble that

I will awake fully baked & arisen like a fresh loaf of bread,
with immense weight off of my shoulders and head,
I AM raised, erected, alive & prepared to take on that mysterious
NEW Day before me, set out to climb a mountain, swim the sea,
with my inner indifference calmed, back in touch with my warm reality,
deeply safe & snug in her arms…with her in mine,
appreciating our every moment in time,
connecting through touch, heart, soul and mind, with so much potential,
so much still to be defined, refined, unleashed, experienced,
for me, for her, for WE & our every natural tendency-

Collectively discovering, a love with the energy of fury, loyalty, romance,
elated & excited to be together
happiness, growing, churning, sharing, expressing,
…wanting ..with such conviction-
Yearning for her & I to have that greatest day
Repeat itself on & on, again & again
making the most of it in the company of my lover & friend,
to have of it what WE wish to make of it,
Finding forgiveness for my epic flawed & failure ridden past
No longer am I slumming into that cold coffin of dishopeful daily doings
pinned beneath the heavy weight of all of my murky & mechanically
malfunctionaratively, discombobulated, limitative excuseful laden means,
continuously or not, sorting myself out for a better fight
as more than just some cube life living dreamer with a pathetic plight,

84

picking through my best of intentions, choosing my best dimensions,
to release me from what is clearly a…-me, myself and I warzone-scenario,
in an untypical, redundantly charged, ever-sustained suspension,
for from my past mistakes I endure seeking some surreal redemption,
burdening my inner vampires with stakes so deep,…with odds so high,

those very odds thwarting me from thriving, grounded, no sky in sight,
whilst I witness a momentary ray of hope, diving in with careful delight,
witnessing myself, momentarily blossoming, expanding, achieving,
though…never the less, that progress reverts, still I continue believing,
while faltering back, losing that wonderful momentum, step by step,
stumbling again over that probable curse of bad luck or self-deceiving,
that same matter of fact that haunts me, that same misfortune that enjoys
those anti-buoyancy battles waged within the heart of I, myself & me;

The Great Escape from the Cube Life

(Back when I was living the Corporate Cube Life, 2008-2013 era)

My aging body is sending me mixed messages and signals,
down those red, white & blue walls within that long & cold hall of pride,
knowing that I am missing out on something out there somewhere,...
though...happy I am that I am not alone, for I have found her....
my friend, my lover, my other, the ONE that I set out to discover,
and still, I am still working on that work in progress..being..Yours truly,
treading carefully through the battlefield of my besieged 3,
striving to grow, believe...while trying to adapt to the changes before me,
with my family & music...being so very valued & adored by me,
avidly taking a stand in my daily coffin like cube
like cell like prison like state of mind-

Understanding that I hold the key to elevate myself out of this place
I often, with hopeless demeanor..find myself within, nailed down by
some assortment of bad decisions that I've made along my way, like sins,
with my dreams & passions in that sparse field of hope
perched up like a two-headed crow to scare off those dark grim
birds that wish to feed upon the crops of my future objectives,
making my heart uneven, squeezing my soul....for remaining here
I can no longer live with my life, my future, no longer in my control..

Though I stand my ground, even when I am feeling down and limited,
seeping into a terrific state of restful release, trying to outsmart my
personal & relevant time piece,
unknowing of how much more of this life I have yet to lease,
while this daily situation fleeces me, worries me, taxing me greatly,
draining me, fooling me...conspiring against me,

enabling me to continue waging war against where I am

& where it is I wish that I could be,

instead of working in this corporate land of non-stop processing,

so daydream I… in daily rotation, about my unfulfilled dreams

with intense frustration, brought on by my own foolish choices…

feeling like I'm no more, no less than being done and through

by the time I exit the doors where I wish to return no more…

. … ; or –what if I tried harder,…if I tried more, if I worked harder,

Made more money, focused more on work, focused less & less

On my lackluster hopes & dreams, allowing my creative talents

Wants & needs …to simply slip through tiny seams,

No longer following those tawdry foolish schemes,

No longer believing in constipated dreams,

Arriving to work each day, to work for a paycheck,

On a remarkable team of co-workers,

No afterhours friendships, no pay raises that my wallet chills,

For I arrive at work, to work, making the money for my bills,

& maybe, if I had any remaining hope & energy, once free from the cube,

I might very well partake in some creative spills & thrills….

Even though I know that I am forever stuck in that redundancy

That shapes my future day by day, controlling me & my fate,

Until I can finally face the Piper, with my plans for that big life change,

When I finally decide to getaway on that great escape,

Even though I know that my dreams may never pay,

It takes abundant courage to set out, living life your own way;

(Thankfully, I was able to flee & be freed from my cube life to try different opportunities 8/2013.

From those cube life pros & mostly cons…I entered yet…another set of pros & cons…As is Life.)

Subject: big weight
Date: Fri, 12 Nov 2010 17:01:26 -0700
Like a Big Weighted Heavy Weight I need to get off my chest.......b4idie

Imagine....as I do...
that which keepith you up so very late, with no sleep at all.......
And if by chance..you are fortunate enough
To catch a wink, you shall only dream about
how your failing & fallen, while some live the dream
I stress & worry about how I may have missed my calling-

So this verbalized form of expression,
writing myself out on pages with total imprecision
this being...my own form of therapy,
so those particles of stress, of & in my life,
don't continue to fall like a heavy snow upon my ego mountain,
possibly causing a most horrific avalanche of emotions-

Like an axe to the soul of my tree, that big weighted heavy weight
keeping me immobile, lacking confidence, unmotivated, fearful,
succumbing daily to that perceptual state of despair & diminishing light
that keepith me up late at night, caught up in a head VS pillow fight,
tossing & turning while my brain gears continuously keep churning,
wishing that I could carefully pull my SELF doubt
out from that frayed power outlet of woeful worryful self-resentments,
experiencing a momentary slumber, waking like a zombie, eyes all blurry,
with my dreams in a rut, while the world around me..moves in a scurry,
I wonder what verdict will leave me vexed, care of myself, judge & jury-

And on any given day, from my past to my current place in time....
a winter storm of widespread stress barrels in with hella flurries,
Once again...I am hung out to dry by my own internal juries,
me, myself & i at war alongside all those real life "shit happens" furies....

Vanquished by my own arsenal of vulnerabilities & timidities
so write I, so rhyme I.. to work out my inner issues,
therapy through words, wrath & bliss infused.......
with so many words, redundancies, emotions,
I apologize if you feel that the author is slightly, or mostly confused....
Though I tread on, line by line, sharing this weight upon, within, my chest
feeling flatly depleted as a modern day failure on a sinking boat of duress
trying 2 figure out what changes are internally needed 4 assured progress,
wondering, if beneath my fleshy composition, " am I sick and bleeding?...
revolving around temporary tangents of self-paranoia
writing is my way of releasing, coping, to hopefully lessen the strain,
keeping myself hopeful, to keep myself trying, to keep my SELF sane...
until I forfeit such rationality due to my world caving in once again-

Turning 40, and my mind and health seem to be receding,
for my daughter, my dreams, my passions, I want 2 live,
I'm not praying for more time, no need to be greedy,
see me now, I'm on my knees, begging & pleading....
As I continue to write, sing, rhyme, rap,
feeling that 99.9 percent of YOU may never give a crap
nor care to find themselves listening or reading
that which I create & share, exuding with conviction,
brooding like a man-baby at times,
So, I'm admitting that I've got a most specific un-unique condition,
& with all of my existing potential, I feel that my overall
central circumference is totally worth understanding

y to this lock, that makes me feel locked down,
this day still growing, searching & finding myself,
as I've been here before, at this very moment in time,
outside this very same door, kneeling,
patience peeling away like old paint,
repeating to myself, "stay awake, I can't afford to faint
nor can I afford any more unfortunate fate"....
finding it easy to say that I can, & easier to feel that I can't,
watching the old me grow older & slower,
hours before I turn that young wiser age of 43, (soon to be 44 on 1/30/15)
while the wise me is still teething,
alive & well weaving my writing gifts through the sands of time

Like spinning my expressive wheels'n'webs in the attic of my imagination
existing in that new corporate cell that I daily dwell to pay the bills,
with ideas & words still surging within me, creating such chills,
creating my history, finding happiness, surviving misery,
this man… & all that makes me whom I am today,
I still find the energy to continue embracing
my creative forces, within every inch of what there is left within me,
choosing to write instead of choosing to bicker & fight,
writing the way I do, with words as my colors, from pink to blue,
with my blood pouring out, soaking the white carpet of these pages,
Covering that same very floor I daily make my daily stand,
as nothing more than some unknown writer,
or just another poet, just another dreamer, just another man ….
& if that is the case, I certainly do understand,
For this life of mine, this life I live….it is my fault,
For I had no set and solid plan in place yesterday,
I can only hope that tomorrow I will find my place,
That place that I belong,

Where I will embrace the world with my heart, soul & mind,
Through expressive word & song,
Not just as a poet, not merely as some unfamiliaritidly befuddled author,
But as all that I am, from my rights to my wrongs,
Living out my destiny, sharing my dreams, discovering new dawns,
In this crazy world of Kings, Queens, Noble Peasants & Pawns,
Dictators, Terrorists, Murders & Thieves, Victims & Villains,
Where the end is most terribly nigh…only if we decide to say goodbye,
So…expressing my heart & soul through the art of poetry choose I,
Instead of waiting it out & silently over boiling up until the moment I die;

Even at my new age of 44, being that I am just but…an hour older..
Whilst editing…tying up this revised book of mine…
I am still involved at times…in those sad battles of me VS me VS life…
Still feeling like a BIG WEIGHT is weighing me down…...
Trying to live…while trying not to drown…;

Without Regret

The smell of sweet passion can vary,
Very well rating & reeking beyond being simply profound,
An aroma unlike any other, a feeling unlike any other,
The smell of sweet accomplishment through being driven & sound-

Whilst he/she whom possesses abundant amounts
Of that special brand of pungently proven pertinent passion
Does so exist to live their lives
Critically, continually, continuously, unconditionally free,
Free to think, Free to dream, Free to be themselves
Unlike unread dusty old books on wobbly wood shelves…

Wreaking, ravaging, raging, ebbing, flowing,
Following dreams with a vastly daring heart on sleeve,
Admitting that they,…that WE.. are not The All Knowing,
While sharing, expressing, showing, to-ing & froing
Creating, Waking, walking, climbing, crawling, trying…
Failing, falling, getting back up with passion undying….

Striving to find the strength to stay focused & hopeful
Through circumstances that range from amazing to awful
Knowing…that WE…

…………………………………………………..must still BELIEVE—

Even if we are loving beggars begging for optimism & happiness
In the cold company of vicious villains, warmongers, killers & thieves....
That WE must continue living in a society that can so easily deceive
Prevailing with copious levels of furiously joyful furious love
Coursing through our every vein & artery....

Like unyielding wolves in a wild winter wonderland
Hunting prey eagerly with sharpened dreams as teeth,
Howling up towards moonlit sky,
OUR Faith, OUR Passion, OUR Hope...
OUR FUTURE..................
....WE shall strive to remain alive....!

Through the horror filled history of a past we cannot forget...

No matter the obstacles, no matter the threat....

We Shall Struggle for a Better Tomorrow, for One & for All, for once & for All...

....Without Regret;

BENEATH A DREARY MOON

Enjoy a cup of comfort
with a teaspoon of tranquility
Under a dreary moon
where something dark & bothersome
Will arrive indeed so very soon
too leave you feeling empty,
numb, & rather consumed
Beneath a Dreary Moon,
where lovers gather,
Where lovers swoon,
where lovers divide
Inside walls of doom,
when true love dies,
When a cup of tea no longer comforts,
when romance no longer gratifies,
once there is nothing more to signify or exhume here,
Beneath a Dreary Moon;

The Mystery of Our Past, Present & Future History,
through the trials, tribulations, truths & lies of our lives.............

Oh How

They Drag Out their Demons line by line, page by page,

Film by film, like dull well paid historical professionals

With countless proud readers within their mandibles

Following, believing, becoming extraordinary crucibles-

So unconcerned, so disconcerting, radicalized & unnerving...

For we can't be sure or not

That 'They' have written Our past & future,

That Doubt...there is no averting,

For only the alterable will allow such an easy converting,

As they continue dissolving & deconstructing decades at a time,

The dark magicians that get off on altering our humankind....

And for that...Separated & divided we will remain

Either Curious, Awake & Aware, speaking out, standing up...

Or uncurious, careless, & selfishly blind-

It's that same old story of Devils VS Angels once again...

It's Our past VS our Future once again...

Creating such an array of tantalizing stories & beliefs

Told thus with climactically wicked intentions

By mostly masculine methodical men

Opening our imaginations up to such ridiculous inventions,

Whilst some righteously follow,

Some of us wonder...

"Are some elements of our history more false than true?"-

They've written as they continue to write...
Words that anger, words that confuse, words that excite
While sharing the who, how, why, where & when
We began, & when we shall end,
While creating for us a world in & of Fear
Awaiting our next plot inducing scare,
Life is life...for it is people that make it unfair-

Using words to romanticize, criticize, enslave, betray,
Words of sarcasm, words of hate,
Words that cause revolts, words of truth, of lies, of power,
Words written by the meek, the strong, the weak, the cowards,
Words that tell us of where we've been & why,
Words of fiery pride that have soldiers signing up to die,
Words that cause confusion, misconstrued, taken out of context,
The power of the almighty word used as a weapon
To incite emotions from joy to rage,
Words that we sadly allow to control our fate-

Some of us follow them, believing each word read, each word heard,
Following along like sheep, like cattle, people in their herd,...
While the sum of some of us deem them as being quite absurd,
Unwilling to continue supporting them and their mission of
Filling books through time with such bitter evil incantations,
Promised promises that seem more
Like vulture culture lies or
Hidden dark little secret alibies,...
Dark spells, dark magic, dark hearts at work
Directing us to turn a page, to burn a page,
To flow against the current, or merge with the undertow....
For the purpose of controlling our massive populate

Like the Puppet Master each puppet show,
In the shoes of an author, writing chapters
That have us starting off as cavemen
In a world with grand sized raptors,
Capturing our history while mixing myth with proof,
Bones with drawings..
Those first uncivilized sprawlings,..

Like a writer develops stories of fantasy & reality,
One idea ending with another, one path crossing another,
Writing our history to simply plot brother VS brother,
with Villains & Victims, Protagonists VS Antagonists,
Heroes & Zeroes, Numbers VS Letters...Characters,
People like you & me..
Living out our destiny created by men both good & bad,
Those men that offer up lots of plots, twists & conspiracies,
Using words on pages to steer society in various directions.....

Controlling the storyline each time,
Shaping the people of the world,
One heart, one mind at a time,
Setting the tone, the landscape, that state of mind
That has us either aware or unknowingly blind,
Sequenced events permeate through our history......

Building conflicts between men,
Directing us to our most unsavory end
With no true resolution in sight
As resolution has become nothing more
Than warring forth & putting up a great fight
Allowing hate to seep deep within our humanity

Contaminating the currents of our society
Deconstructing the way we distinguish between wrong & right
Creating a disastrous Darkness within our subconscious
Which decreases our loving Light within
Our compassion & consciousness,
Through words, books, fairytales, history tales,
Actual events that have been spun by wordsmithing word spinners,
Those that contribute mounds of bullshit like well versed sinners,
Those that we put great trust in,
Unable to truly discern if what has been written & rewritten,
Is fact or mere breached fiction, by being corrected & re-corrected
By men that claim to speak for a Being of Higher Power,
Breeding & using both power & fear
To keep the flock reading & following close & near,
While some of us wonder if what has been written is faithful truth…
Or merely some fabricated fairytale
That keeps us hoping for Heavenly grace
While we dwell in a world where Hell consumes our space
In a World…where we base our lives, beliefs & religions
On what has been created by a collection of writers with perhaps
Large egocentric erections that get off on writing our history
From our start to our end,

Or are they nothing more than mere imaginatively creative men
With powerful minds & wealthier friends,
That worship power & money before people & gods,
That very power & wealth that allowith them to control our very
Vulnerable past, present & future existence,
While feeding lines of lies with words that blind hearts & minds
While dividing woman & man between the destitute & opulence fulfilled,
Right here, where Good battles Evil with such a loathed resilient appeal…

Chalking it up to this ...

    If LIFE were no more than a basket of eggs,

    A basket made by man, weaved with truth or lies,

    If that were the case,

    Should we follow the flow of that manmade undertow,

    Stick to their plot, stew in their boiling pot,

Or not?....

    Knowing that not everything is as it seems,

We continue to survive by allowing

Various Villains & Heroes to vividly haunt our lives & dreams...

    Controlling Our lives by somehow

    choosing who lives, choosing who dies....

    Whilst we dig through the ruble of our history

    Trying to differentiate between each page of truth & lies,

    Creatively Concocted, page by page, line by line…

    Within those books that were constructed & written

    To keep humanity in line,

    To simply help us get through this experience

    That they've conveniently named Life?;

The River of Life & Death, Dreams & Realities

The rapid river is all together....
disaster & beautiful splendor...
and everything in between...
to each one something different it doth mean,

That ever flowing river of life & death, dreams & realities
where anything can happen, from joyful moments to tragedies,
That mysterious river that can get you there, someplace, somewhere,
or leave you bewildered, stranded & unprepared,
that much colder & closer to nowhere....
or it may drown you with its quick & gripping ripping currents
while you are in pursuit of dreams or schemes for
change or things like that
that do so happily or sadly occur for sure
whether your heart is dark, lost,
fulfilled, spiteful, loving or pure
the rapidness of progress can overturn
you on your river quest,
wearing & stripping you down from your best
to your worst, living out your own personal curse,..
from a living dreamer to just another dead
cold body at the bottom of that river bed,
no longer flowing down through what could be
known as an endless river of dreams, lived & unlived,
unknown, unchartered, unmapped,
with talent that could so go untapped
within each willing soul, that river moves us or take a precious toll...
and you must be willing to dive on in, to take that ride,

no longer from that eerie chill of fear
you can unwillingly hide,
no longer to those rules and normal standards
you are willing to abide,
for that river ride comes down to
dreaming, living, or dying while trying
before the river bends, before the river ends,
for when you die, there is no trying again,
so know that the River is not your enemy, nor your friend,
It is just a device, a path, a direction to head
Unless you sink to its deep, dark river bed
by quitting when you should have been living instead;

HEAVEN IS HELL WITHOUT YOU!

Loneliness is a gun,
the days without you here, are the bullets,
Hope is the safety,
Sadness is the hammer,
I just want to throw this gun away,
I just want to hear you say, "Found am I, found by you".
This heaven is hell, without you, hell is hotter than usual,
without you, heaven just isn't the same.

Here I am, with this Gun of loneliness against my fragile heart,
splitting me upside down, inside out
with fears that play their part,
I viewed those mug shots of people like you and me
beautiful women & men, that caused such devastating tragedy,
thinking that you can't see it all in the face of one,
that someone that could be right today,
with contagious attitude,
could be very well wrong tomorrow,
wrong with savagery, from sharing love, to sharing sorrow;

I don't want a bombshell or someone ready to explode,
I only want to find one available wonderful woman,
to know, allowing our friendship to grow,...

A woman that wants to take the time on our relationship
between her and I, as I would call out to the world
screaming happily, "She's the One",
and I'd be her guy, as she screamed, "He's the one for me";

Seeking…..
Something found with sweet apple scents,
strawberry delights, fulfilling our lovely loving appetites…

Something we both would only deny if we continued to be
locked down in this online world-
where texting and emails, posts and profiles with pics
Facebooking networking cookies for nookies,
just don't satisfy the true at heart, …..
so many people, some fake as hell,
though here so many happily dwell,
here, where people forget how to expressively reply or respond,
thinking that we know it all,
but we only know the moon provides us light on such a
beautiful night, as we take that first walk,
leaving behind the frantic, manic online world,
on a tightrope of chance,
on the ballroom floor awaiting our first expressive slow dance,
with roses at your fingertips and such sweet adequate reasons,
the best of our own internal seasons,
seasonings, ingredients, coming together,
this is our day in the park, our picnic perfect weather….

Hopeful for a final ascent,
for that find in this chilling online world
where so many are fixated on visuals,
yet so very deaf & blind to expression, passion, & communication
exhausted by lies, cheats,
for a fresh new start is due,
with pleated cleaner sheets;

An act of hot, spicy, juicy sex may blow a gust of wind into your sails,

but so much more is needed to sail the seas of one fine relationship

with one fine person, during this one fine very short lifetime.

Tossing that gun of loneliness into the depths where oil creeps up

like a vicious monster set free from the bottom,

creating a modern day date mate city like Gomorrah & Sodom,

as in life, pain and happiness we are swiftly dealt,

so that we may perhaps appreciate what we feel,

and what we have felt,

so why not deal with life with someone in your corner,

someone beside you, to hold, to love, to share,

to color rainbows with,

to survive the storms, ups and downs, changes,

the abnorms to norms

to care for, to adore, to endure this damn

crazy most beautiful life with,

instead of without,

for my heaven....is Hell,

for this hell could be heaven if you were here with me,

my friend, my lover, my one and only.....

oh where, ...could you be;

The Failure & the Growth within the worst to best of me

What flowed through my mind this morning…
shortly after I awoke, while putting away dishes…
was this that I do now confess….,
How pathetic it does feel, when your past mistakes..
and any mistakes you've made, from the start to the present…
can continue to haunt you, ripping and tearing you down-

Tearing down you, yourself, your relationship, your future…
as you ponder, wondering where you'll end up,
or when the road will open up and swallow you hole,
heart, mind, creativity, imagination, dreams, body & soul-

Noticing in that moment…
just how Failure Friendly I've been, & still am,
And that which remains of my internal hope,
dimly dwindles while I feel that I'm feeling rather self-damned,….
At least I can honestly admit that denial doesn't drink from my cup…
Owning up to each excuse & event that has shaped my life,
my past, my present & my future,
my failures…which equal my growth…
thinking with hammerous intent…
that I am where I am, below the goals I had wished for
but perhaps..I haven't work hard enough, long enough to achieve
…knowing…deep down…that I'm here…
because it is & has always been…and will remain to be
the blame of that battle that rages within, myself & me
while I unsparingly & admittedly announce denounce-fully
…..that this Failure of Me…. is….

My fault..
My situation,
My place,
My debt,
My doubts,
My life,
My loss,
My struggle,
My choice,
My excuse,
My crutch,
My weakness,
My bleakness,
My self-condemnation,
My frustration,
My awful mistake,
My worst,
My curse………..

My own historically pathetic atmosphere that continues to absorb
a continuous flow of mistakes, issues, downs,
no matter how high I hold my head,
When your past mistakes keep coming back to haunt you
per every new bump in the road, mistake, foul up….
then well…at the moment you are at war with the current mistake…
all the rest decide to attack…making it harder…
on your life, your dreams, relationships…..

Feeling more like a plane about to crash,
A ship about to sink,
A lost dreamer on the brink of dreams about to end
Before they were even ever able to begin-

Wishing there was a big enough rock to curl up under..
To hide beneath, hiding all of my flaws & blunders
While wishing that I could erase those passions within me
That keep me hopeful, hopeless, driven, growing, striving,
Trying, ...yet...dolefully denying...that I will never finish
Anything that I've set out to accomplish
For the sake of fulfilling my own wild-eyed dreams,
Unless I can choose to believe that my failures are meant to be,
A sign of something better that will come of me-

Sadly & soberingly....I do so deserve what is before me,
Staring back at me from the reflection of each cup, each plate,
Each being a reminder of my life & each of my unfilled destinies,
Wondering if the answer to my growth is due to each of my calamities
Clashing in the frigid soil of my checkered history
Along with each of my issues pointing out
Every excuse of my semi-negative state of hopeless doubt,
As I dare to admit each of my many insecurities out loud, semi-proud
Of each beautiful highlight, each moment of strife,
Each stone thrown at my glass house,
Each cut caused by the vile veracity of life,
From my triumphant efforts to my relevant tears that ever
So foolishly drown-out my varied skeptical tragedies
Within that overall design of my worst to best parts of me-

These are my Dark Strides, my cynical progressions,

Out in the open with no place to hide

Where my Darkness & my Light unifiably reside....

To poetically declare the story of my life, my wrongs, my rights

Each beautiful attempt, each failure,

Each part of my heart, my soul,

Each dream I've lost,

Each dream I've found,

Out in the open with no place to hide,

Sharing myself in words,

Both, my horridly expressive side, & my charmingly profound side,

Meeting in the center of myself & my Vague & Vivid Variations, again";

This Thankful Heart of Mine,...

Rememberith..that WE are All allowed to Shine again, after each storm

My Brother, My Sister, My Mother, Rest in Peace My Father,

My Friend, My Family...each & every one within Humanity,

Fellow Thinker, Fellow Dreamer-

Thank You so much for YOUR time,

Thank You so much for reading

Those words that my heart enjoyed expressively bleeding,

Thank YOU so much for YOUR acquisition of my book..

For these words are mere ingredients, & I am the baker, I am the cook,

Baking & Cooking up what I do hope your eyes & heart did surely adore,

& if so, please do know that there is more of me to explore

If that reading quest you can of course endure-

**THANK YOU SO MUCH FOR YOUR AWESOME SUPPORT!

To: Brian Oakley & Madison! YOU ROCK! for being the 1st to purchase my

first 2 cd/book bundle! Being my Dark Strides II book,

& both of my cd self-releases-my WrathBliss' Beauty Beneath the Beast EP

& my We Are Hip Hop Humans! explicit hip hop mixtape, W.A.H.H.H!

Wishing anyone that has or hasn't read my words...

ALL the best in & of Life, Love, Laughter,

Dreams, Goals, Happiness, Relationships, Peace & Etc;

My daughter D.R.....I believe in you. Dream, Live, Become YOU!

My love O.M...Our 1st chapter is great... the rest will be greater!

My mom Genivee, You deserve so much! Love YOU!

To my Son, We are so happy to have you here with us.

We look forward to your first words, interests, & beyond!

Love Dad & Mom

Furthermore....

To My Daughter, My Son, My Love, My Friend, My Family & You:

Do what you love, do what you dream, sooner than later-

Do it with love, do it for you, be strong

& unto yourself, always remain respectful & true,

Even if no one notices who you are

Or what you've created during your time,....

You'll know that you loved, that you lived,

That you truly were an inspiration,

Because you tried, even when you were weak & tired,

Making the most of it all, before your time here expired-

So for now...this is where my book shalt sweetly END...

UNTIL YOUR EYES & MY WORDS

Calmly COLLIDE together on pages Once again...

Hopefully before our World & our Lives, our Dreams reach an end;

Wishing you ALL a most Happy New Year 2015 & Beyond & Above,

Filled with Laughter, Understanding, Patience,

Respect, Hopes, Dreams, Peace & Love-

Sincerely,

Wrathbliss aka Timothy D.M

Be it wrong or be it right....

This is where my dark & light do clash tonight,

No matter what...

As Frank said,

"I did it my way",

Or...

As Limp Bizkit Fred said,

"I'm 'a do things my way, It's my way, or the highway"

For I am imperfectly perfect & here to stay!

Save Us from Ourselves, on Earth...in Hell

Dear God, Dear Powers that BE, Dear UNIVERSE,

We...the BELIEVERS, the HOPEFUL...are going on strike!

    & We admit that WE did it, that WE took it for granted,

        That WE ruined it, That we broke it,

            WE admit that ..though we've tried,

                WE just can't better it, heal it, fix it.....

Our world, our society, our hopes, our lives, our dreams...are suffering...

& since you won't HELP, We the hopeful believers... are giving up,

We are looking for our Savior, our father, our mother, our angel

Because we can no longer continue down this path at this pace

The spiraling down of our entire history, our entire human race.....

In a world of so much beauty...there is so much hate & tragedy...

Though we continue to strive for something better for our humanity...

With so much ignorance, fear, terror, greed, deceit, murder & loss

WE are growing more & more wearied, confused, forgotten & lost

In a society that gainfully cultivates more & more sadistically sullen folks

Pitting Believers against Non-Believers, Haves VS Have Nots

Religion VS Religion, Man VS Man, People VS Planet, Fear VS ALL, ...

So...Please HEAR US...WE know that OUR chronic circumstances

Are OUR own FAULT, our history of war, violence, crimes against ALL..

And WE are so very tired of believing, hoping, working for a

Positive change, a better society, a better future, a stronger resolve...

As WE so sincerely admit, that we have far too many problems to solve

Before WE can ever truly ascend, escaping our self-created ill fate,

WE must be shown how to finally..truly evolve, free from spite & hate,

So...Please...Please..HELP US!!!!!, SAVE OURSELVES from Ourselves;

I AM, I AM NOT...

This is my dedication...A slight dedication...
A mere long ramble...regarding that cold current event...
That took place this week,
That has humanity looking at itself again,
Taking more than a quick gander
At the state of our society, indifferences & differences alike-

Our FREEDOMs, Our FEARs, Our Unity, Our Community..
And how a satirical publication ..like...Charlie Hebdo,
Became a victim to an act of Terroristic Extremism-

Another tragic event where unarmed human lives
Are lost to those well-armed selfish few....
A dark disaster that has left many people grieving,
A reminder of how precious...& how dangerous
Freedom of expression truly is,
That very FREEDOM that should be FOUGHT for...
With Love, with Laughter, Hope, Peace & Understanding...
While those many EXTREMISTs sit around demanding
That WE DIE!!!, while descanting
That we are worth killing & murdering in the name of religion-

Reminding us of just how tainted religion has become
And has continued to be through our short but long existence,
With all the crusades, killings, the slaughtering of humankind
That has occurred throughout our history of vengeful violence
Our FREEDOM of Expression..You Will Never SILENCE;

Wouldn't it be dandy if we could end
That evolving Extremist mentality, hate, war, violence, racism?
As well as the need to share Antagonizing & provoking
Cartoons that mock, poke fun at, make fun of
People, Prophets, Figures that are followed, feared, loved, praised-

Can't we become a better society without that type of behavior
Between one another, between brother & brother
While still expressing our hearts & thoughts with eventful variety
Without stirring up the hornets' nest
By putting down people & their religiousness, beliefs, differences,
Hurting people, causing them to retaliate none the less…
For even satirical humor can pack a punch with a bitter bite-

Satirical sarcasm can be seen as having such a spiteful might
Of ill convictions & bad intentions that can offend & smite
Causing more division between people that leads to a fight,
Where one side uses satirical humor to express themselves,
& the other side incites violence to avenge themselves-

Though….
What has just taken place on the streets of Paris,
Is a great example of how viciously horrid people can be
When fueled by such selfishly sadistic, extremist beliefs
Be this and example, a notice to all…
That Extremism on any level
For any God, for any Prophet, for any belief at all
Is no better than working for & with that big horned, tall,
Cruel & twisted, callous, inhuman, unconscionable Devil-

No matter your belief, group, race or religion,

Extremism is a dark force of a few VS FREEDOM for ALL,

Extremism is ignorance blanketed with coldblooded hate,

Extremism is awful & horrid, the way cowards retaliate,

Extremism seems to fill our history, page by page

Of deaths, murders, wars, violence and rage,

Fighting over everything & anything possible,

As if LIFE & Human Lives have forever been deemed

Un-meaningful, unimportantly unviable

As Villains have sought Victims out to end their survival,

Ending lives based on holy stories that incite war & rage,

Those same words that are praised by the rank & file,

Living their lives by the suggestions of that Manmade Bible

Expecting that much more from their life experience,

Becoming judge, jury & executioner,

While trying to earn holy points with the Grand Inventor

While we continue down our dark path of division

Dividing hearts, souls, minds, families, nations

In a world where EVIL & LIGHT

Are in constant conflict, day & night,

While each member of society

Must decide, "on which side shall I fight, wrong or right"

Wondering if their right is more wrong,

Or is their wrong…more right-

Whilst there are many that could care less

About our future,….about our progress,

With no sense of compassion, with no sense of humor,

Those that believe strongly in taking lives, killing, murdering,

Slaughtering anyone for anything, in the name of vengeance
Believing that such acts are above all righteous & splendid,
For entrance to a Heavenly Paradise is what's intended,
No matter how many lives must be murdered & taken…..

Praised by those that believe in the same,
Believing that it would be a distinguished honor
To forever be remembered in the belly of the martyrs flame,
Feeling great pride for taking so many lives shamelessly
With no shame to share, no shame to hide,
Believing that avenging through vengeful violent heights
Makes them & their rampage of death nothing but right..

For I am SICK of this state of mind…..or anything like it….
that which causes many to join those dark forces,
throwing our world into the dark ages
of sinful & senseless killings once again….
saying….,
"In the Name of……, I will avenge my God,
My Prophet, my Family, my Country…
Killing them all, cartoonists and all, comedians & all,….
Anyone that stands up with an opinion,
Anyone with a different belief,
Anyone that denounces me, Anyone that wants FREEDOM-

Anyone that stands against us,
Anyone that wants a better world,
Anyone that uses blasphemy,
Anyone that is not ME….Death to YOU!"

Sarcasm can be hurtful…
Satire can be harmful…
But it should not carry a murderous death sentence!!

Furthermore, unarmed teens should not be murdered in the streets
By the police, their peers, or any human beings-

People should not be killing other people, PERIOD!

Yet…this dark pattern of misfortune continues to needle its way
Through the heart of our society, through the fabric of our day,
Because humans cannot all be on the same page of peace, love,
Equality, respecting one another…No…of course not.
That would be too hard to accomplish, though we pray for it.
So we suffer & survive, some together, many divided…….
In a world where there is so much anger, so much deceit,
So much disgust, ignorance, so much hate, so much rage
Being directed against one another due to our diverse beliefs-
Brother against brother, father against father,
White VS Black, Black VS White, Police VS Civilian,…
Civilian VS Police, Christian VS Muslim, Man VS Man,
Government VS Citizen, Power VS People,
Warlord VS Innocent, Death VS Life, Dark VS Light,
The armed & violently wrong VS the unarmed & peacefully right;

Not all police, politicians, people…are corrupt, evil, dark,
     greedy, conniving & willing
To live their lives doing nothing but hurting, raping, stealing,
     being misleading, corrupting & killing…

NO!!! REALLY!!!!

Not every man is against every man…

Not every passionate person passionate about their beliefs

Is EXTREME ENOUGH to kill for their beliefs..

Not every man is racist, believing that his race is supreme,

Not every man uses satire & sarcasm to battle demons,

Not every man is hateful,

Not every man is out for blood,

Not all Men are ferocious, dark, malicious, avaricious, vindictive,

Caught up in such vicious circles of unflinching violent acts-

NO!!!...for there are good people in the world…

Great PEOPLE….Loving, Caring, Compassionate….

With something to say, something to share,

And we won't always get it,

And we won't always agree,

And though we have our differences…

There is a beauty that can be found in our commonalities….

The biggest one of all being…We Are Alive…

And WE ARE

Able to forgive, Able to think,

Able to resist that feeling that drives us to hate,

Able to stop the Violence,

Able to LOVE,

Able to UNDERSTAND,

WE ARE…YOU ARE…

Able to stop hurting & killing PEOPLE like me, PEOPLE like you

Because they are of a different color and/or culture,

Because they believe in a different Religion, God, Prophet,

Raised on different Beliefs,

OR maybe…

Because they don't believe in religion,

Because they are not like you ..or me…or us, or them,…

Because they do that which smites you, that which offends…

Strip us of our differences & beliefs….and we are all the same….

We ALL wish to Live Out our time

Experiencing this rather short, precious life

Knowing that we could fall victim to disease,…

Or some natural..instant death could possibly occur..

Knowing that a lifetime of sickness could grip us…

So why must WE continue KILLING each other…..

In the name of………..who, what, when & where…

WHY must so many continue to die…

For the purpose of such cowardly vengeance;

My condolences to all the families that have lost loved ones

In the name of, for the reason of…

Terror, hate, indifference, ignorance, extremism,

Greed, darkness, the evils that some men do ….

Those senseless tragedies caused

By those vengeful creatures that put Gods, Prophets,

& Profits…before People like me & you;

-Life is Beautiful..and it is at times, Chaotic & Dangerous-

& I hope all the gold, treasures, diamonds, virgins & praise

That you have or do hope to yield…

In that holy, heavenly paradise of tranquil fields,

 …where you seem to want to forever reside…

Were truly worth all the lives that you chose to murder & kill,

The grief you caused, the blood you spilled…

For there is truly no greater form of foolish egotism

Than that plight that ends Humanity in a bloody fight;

I AM A HUMAN,

I HAVE PASSIONS,

BELIEFS,

EMOTIONS,

DREAMS,

ISSUES,

VALUES,

MORALS,

DOUBTS,

FEARS,

FRUSTRATIONS,

WORRIES,

IDEAS,

FAULTS,

INSECURITIES,

BEAUTY,

DEPTH,

CONSCIENCE,

TALENT,

PURPOSE,

I AM NOT A MURDERER of HUMANS;

-People are wonderful, until they become cruel, evil & vengeful-

The Ingredients of Me, Myself & I

From my worst to my best
I am part.......
Enthusiast, Opinionist,
Protagonist, Antagonist,
Mellowdramaist, Determinist,
Fatalist, Pessimist, Survivalist,
Eccentrist, Eclectist, Nomadist,
Ramblist, Poeticalist, Pianist, Apprehensionist,
Humorist, Explorist, Sensationalist,
Romanticist, Spiritualist, Improvist,
Loyalist, Procrastinist, Rebellist, Compassionst,
Self-Deprecatist, Rationalist, Parentalist, Connectionist,
And All Humanist -
At War with my greater Optimist,
My Enemy, My Foe,
Warring for hope & good fortune,
Warring for more confidence,
Struggling over worries, failures, finances, fading dreams.......

(As many do, like me, like you)

& from further inner conflict I do hope to resist,
For I seek peace within my heart, soul & mind,
For being matted in inner mêlées is no way to spend one's lifetime-
So here I share my salientative, raw'n'flawed style of word & rhyme,
Greatly Thankful to YOU for your cherished reading time;

To War from within=
To Strive, To Try,
To Fail, To Grow, To Forgive,
To Dream, To Believe, To Live;

Say I, "Bah-Humbug"

With a shoulder shrug,
For I be a temporary slave to self-failure,
Stuck like an old tick drying up in a dirty thick Rug,
Or maybe...something else.., for at times I feel
Like a turtle on his back awaiting a heart attack,
For when I do meet the end of my time,
I will live on through these pages of words & rhyme,
For I know that when I am buried, long & gone...
Life, war, pain, pleasure, beauty, sadness, madness,
Strangers, family, friends, dreamers...will continue on;

In the dim territory of one's self
There is hope...There is a veiled confidence deep down—
Even through inner conflict, it can be found,
As I have found within my own Dark Strides,
Within the chaos of each conveyed page, line by line,
Where the frame of my mien is unique & profound,
At least to this willing participant of humankind;

SOME REDUNDANCIES EXPOSED

Here dear reader are
Some WORDS that were possibly, mightily & widely,
& so very tritely used within this poetical offering of mine...
I did give fair warning regarding the redundant
Redundancies that redundantly exist within these
Here pages of my Dark Strides III- Partial Memoir-ish publication....
(That there...is a rather annoying example of a wordy ranting ramble...)

DUSK, DAWN, AS, GOD, THANK YOU, EXPRESSIVE,
ME, MYSELF, I, WAR, BATTLE, POETICAL,
DREAMING, TRYING, LIVING, END,
SELF-DEPRECATIVE, WARRING, DREAMER, DREAM,
FOR, WHILST, WHILE, &, AND, CASE,
HEART, SOUL, MIND,
LIFE, LOVE, DEATH, DARK, DARKNESS, LIGHT,
WITHIN, THAT, PEACE, ..., ..., .., ...,
Hope, Hopeful, Failure, Failures, Fear, Hell, Heaven, Above, Through,
WrathBliss...

Those are just a few x 10 or so examples of my wordy redundancies...

Hopefully you found meaning, emotion, heart & soul
Within those many words I tied together
In word equations of expressive flow-

Thank you again, for your Time & Consideration,
Be you a stranger, family, distant acquaintance or a close friend,
This is now, for sure, without a doubt,....

In ...My Dark Strides...

down below my optimistic glow,
that is where my confidence hides,
there, where my lack of follow through is felt,
is where my frustration complicates my simplicity,
is where I am most vulnerable,
right where I am most alive,
right where my hope encounterith my hopelessness,
where I fail to pick up the pen and complete
that which should already have found an end
so that I could finally feel that momentum
to start once again,
proudly and passionately...editing, writing, editing,...
readying my writings for that nightmare of self-publishing...
knowing that...I might just be my own worst & best critic...
and the only reader of those words that I've placed
on pages that are sadly lonely with only my eyes
watching from start to finish,
pages that turn, becoming nothing more than blemishes between lines..
and yes... I am greatly aware that I am just another
rambling poet exposing himself with such preposterous prose in a world of
millions upon millions of poetic cons & pros
along with billions of readers
with very few being interested in what comes next...
through that itself...
I must still find the power within me to be resilient as possible...
for my words aggravate even I,
& expressing them...writing them ..is one thing..
but proofreading & editing on my own,
be it ..more cost effective than hiring a pro to do such an important duty......
It is yet another grueling battle that I bitterly hate
To take part in,
For it would be much easier to express my offerings,
line by line,
Then quickly discard them,
one page at a time,
each word expressed being
a most vulnerable key to my heart, soul & mind,
spewed across pages where a few possible readers
might just spend a small amount of time
skimming through my poetic prose,
unknowing that I am the most poetical prose mind of all time;

The FREEDOM of Release

Free to Write...Free to Release...Free to Express myself...my way..
not as you ..and them...might suggest.
Free to explore dreams, thoughts, particles of my reality, sharing my hope,
my hopelessness, ...spewing, ridiculously crafted
rambling word equations...but...really...I should digress, for what I share is
nothing compared to the great poetic minds nor the unknown
poets of humankind...
For many of us find a joy in writing out our hearts in between lines,
like you...like me, we that find Freedom in Writing...even though what is
shared could be deemed, perceived ...as no more than free and dumb,
..or perhaps..for those reading eyes..just a few, maybe you,..
Could very well find these words to be more like..Free and Yummy,
receiving these words like jellybeans and donuts, never mind the diet,
for I write freely, stirring things up with a most sensitive rambling riot,

or maybe..I should have remained silent,
more typical & compliant,
the way many want us to be, uncurious, afraid & quiet;

Such as I

There is no shortage of poets and writers,
There is no shortage of warriors and fighters,
There is no shortage of people and places,
There is though, only one thinker, only one writer, such as I-

    There is no shortage of words that rhyme,
    There is no shortage of sharing minds,
    There is no shortage of thin walked lines,
    There is though, a shortage of precious time-

I speak with words, rhyming, in and out of time,
Confessing, expressing, releasing my heart, soul & mind,
And I know that I'm certainly not the most educated,
And I know that I'm certainly not the most poetic,
And I know that I'm certainly not the pick of the litter,
For I am not the best of the best of the best,
But for these gifts I have to share, I am happily blessed,
For you may care to read on and discover more of me,
Or you can seek out another writer of better poetry-

    No matter what you decide, today or morrow,
    I'll still write my books, be them unread, be I found in sorrow,
    I am expressing my feelings with these fine words that I borrow,
    Like it or leave it, skim it or read it,
    Want it or Need it,
    Here I will write, Here I will sit,
    And at the end of my ramble,
    I will happily quit;

Beauty Beneath the Beast

Will you trouble yourself to
Find the Beauty *Beneath this* Beast *of me*
where my heart is more enticing than my fleshly un-beauty.......
Whilst it is easier to judge a cover too easily for so many,
Could you understand this man that I be
If you could see inside of me,
Here, within our mutual reality-

Where wrong at times out does the right,
Where chance can be the key to fulfilling a destiny...
Right where you will discover the
Beauty Beneath this Beast of Me,
This imperfect man that I am,
Being both blessed & damned,
For the greater good I stand
With my blood on each page,
With pen in my hand,
Whether or not you care to understand,
I am passionate Beast,
I am Loving man;

PEOPLE LIKE ME   PEOPLE LIKE YOU

Walking on a thinning line within the egg of circumstantial chance,
Reaching out to the world from my own world of obscurity-

With each flaw, with each attempt, each insecurity on my sleeve
Like a round pulsating target pulsing with hope,
I continue onward, upward, falling from time to time, down below,
Persevering, trying to keep up, trying to believe...
That there is something more out there for us, for you, for me
Besides the turbulence of this tumultuous sea of dreadful density,
Where we daily find our residence with such bitter propensity-
Trying to escape from those moments of disdain, heartbreak & pain
While appreciating the beauty around us, within us,
Broadcasting our words through channels of chaos
Where listeners listen in a scurried hurry
While I share what I love with tender fury,
Humiliated, hanging from the branches of my own perpetual
Tree of rhyme, losing time, aging somewhere between
Gracefully & Insipidly, falling through fragile cracks, unheard,
Unread, unknown, a familiar story shared by many...
or a few
Painters, songwriters, poets, dreamers,
people like me,
people like you,
unknown, undiscovered by many unlike those famous few,
We exist, we create, we share, yes we do,
Not for worldwide fame & golden egg spoils,
But because People like me & you, to our passions WE are true
To our dreams, to our artful visions, WE are loyal;

88....Keys

I have ...

88 reasons to never give up,

88 poems for you & the world,

88 I Love You',

88 smiles,

88 prayers,

88 kisses,

88 hugs,

88 cuddles,

As I play upon my 88 Keys,

For I have 88 chances,

88 Dreams to share,

88 Fresh Starts for you and I,

& 88 Keys to your Heart,

Each key a day,

Each octave a week,

And when I'm done playing those 88 Keys for You & Me

I will start again, playing for you & I & the world, sweet melodies

Pouring out my heart, mind & soul,

Won't you listen please...

While I share a most sweet release......

On my 88 Keys;

I COMMUNICATE i

I am more than some Dim Dawned Dyhopian (hopeless person) in a dumbed down dystopia,

Creating my own fruitful future from a history of ill violence & sin; for I enjoy

Writing, exciting the SENSES with my own unique poetic prose calling card,

Being that I am no more than some unknown poet with dark to light heart

In a society that doth hath a rich abundant supply of artful bards

With words that hum like birds singing with loud & delightful barge,

Wish I to be my own man, my own writer, without being compared to all the rest,

For I wish to be greater than one that considerith himself to be one of the best,

This ONE writer of poetic rambles, that which is me, writing as I do, raw, expressive & free-

Writing & Writing, rambling & rambling, while understanding that..to try, to create, to share

Is just as dangerous…just as frightening, for it is gambling with your life, hopes & dreams-

Opening yourself up, your world up…to inevitable self-criticism,

And once you are done with doubting yourself, finally believing in yourself,

Finally accomplishing that accomplishment that be so very important to yourself,

Winning the battle of Yourself VS YOU…

Finally..getting yourself out there, your book, your music, your idea, your work of art, of heart

Knowing that soon enough…there will be People, many ..or a few,

To pick you apart, to push you back down, happily obliged to judge you

Since you gave them the opportunity…because you had to follow your dreams, with a price-

Because you finally…believed in yourself enough to no longer procrastinate, give in, give up,

Because you finally understand…with a wiser heart, a wiser soul, knowing the consequences-

You can't please everyone, & YOU can't please yourself….all of the time….

You CAN try, You CAN dream, You CAN create, You CAN express, You can LIVE

Without worrying about whether or not you are better or worse, held back by a curse,

Because once you share your heart & mind, with flaws & all,

You should know that you did what so many people wish that they themselves could do….

Hindered by fear, by that deep & hurtful thought of being ridiculed, rejected …or overlooked

That chance YOU took to share YOURSELF with the People of the World…

No matter how you were received, treated, bypassed, appreciated, or judged,

You did it…knowing all the pros & cons, You did what you loved, You Communicated YOU;

Genetically Modified Wicked World

We live in a wicked world,

For on the nightly news fear & terror does unfurl-

We keep discovering more & more about how

WE have managed to allow material things, money & things,

To outweigh the value of life that we should have for all living beings-

We live a wicked world at war for a wide range of reasons,

While connivers, war mongers & deceitful leaders

Lead us through more questionable seasons

Of murder, vengeance & violence, our voices they try & silence,

Burying us in blankets of fear,

More intent on expansion, making more money,

Getting bigger, stronger, wealthier, stepping over the less fortunate...

Never mind the lives that are lost along the way,

In this wicked world where we still dream of better days...

If it weren't for those that continue to poison us, mislead us, fool us,

Tempt us, control us, divide us...

Then maybe we could do more than just merely imagine ourselves living

In a healthier world where we could enjoy

This gift of life without so much deceit, greed, hate & strife

Stabbing at us like some lunatic with a knife;

THE END of MY Dark Strides III!!!!!!!!

FINALLY!!! Progress at Last!

Thank you for reading my Dark Strides!

-Always remember...that in darkness, there is a light, Your Light-

Additional Gratitude

For sharing Your

COMMENTS, WISDOM, Laughter, Conversation, KINDNESS & SUPPORT,

& for perhaps…buying my book of poetic rambles, music and/or telling people about my creative offerings…

In no specific order

Dean Taylor,   Jimmy Watson,   Victoria Tuckwell,

Gretchen Crowe,   Brett DeLockroy,   Dawn R Berg,

Luis Ruiz,   Marilynn Brower,   Frank N Beans,

Sonny Nicks,   Chris Rodriguez,   Patsy Munoz,

Adan Mares,   Tiffie Pink,   Jessica Rodriguez,

Elise Haagenson,   Mohammed Lateef, Kami Martin,

Joshua Cabrales, Lindsay Rairdon, Danny Lee,

Marcos Bina, Tami Berry-Brock, Deejay illix,

Jorge Arellanes, Angel Cuellar, Marie L Cuellar,

Tracey Maddux Gorbett, Zorica Curkovic, Jai Blanco,

Laura Altobelli, Jeff Barillaro aka Soldier Hard,

Manuel Long, Jana Pink James, Brian Oakley & Madi,

Chris & Melanie Gray,   Audrey Milligan,   John Follis,

Amy Stoeckl Ybarra,   Carrie Langgard, Yolanda Begay,

Suzanne Salladin, Tricia Taylor, Ed Lundell, Lopez Brenda,

Marcel, Julox & All at Angelo's of Aurora, CO,

Chris Ritter, Bruce Stout, Tanisha Robinson, Ben Folds,

Bubbs Esparza, Angel Gonzalez, Angel Cabrales,

Vanessa Bruiser Ragland, Judith Coe, Pablo Fransisco,

Mishelle Findlay-Le, Vanessa Hollingshead, Megan Moon,

Amanda Madden, Carin Dawn, Betty Reta & Oscar,

Chris Melendes, Paula Moses-Hoang, Madison

& Matt & The J FAM, Kay & Roger & Audrey,

& anyone I may have forgotten to mention, TY2!

Grand Gratefulness to my most Beloved:

My Love Orla & our son Finn Timothy,
My mother Genivee R. McAllen,
My daughter DeLanna Rose-

I LOVE YOU ALL SO VERY MUCH!

And Universal Thanks To:

Spirituality,
Love,
Peace,
Understanding,
Respect,
Chance,
Equality,
Our God/Gods,
& the Powers that Be,
Our Universe,
Our Humanity,
Our Existence;

******Why did I end on Page 133? 3 + 3= 6..per the darkness, 6+1= Lucky 7, per the light!*******

Life consists of Bad & Good, Dark & Light…& everything in between. We choose which path, which side to follow daily;

CPSIA information can be obtained
at www.ICGtesting.com
Printed in the USA
LVHW090759040423
743361LV00035B/1772